THE MATCHLESS GIFT FOR UNIVERSAL PEACEFUL LIFE

A. Debachandra Singh

The Matchless Gift for Universal Peaceful Life

BY

A. Debachandra Singh

Copyright © A. Debachandra Singh 2023

Originally Published In India

ISBN: 978-93-95773-58-4

Printer: **RIGI PRINTERS**

Published by RIGI PUBLICATION

777, Street no.9, Krishna Nagar

Khanna-141401 (Punjab), India

Website: www.rigipublication.com

Email: info@rigipublication.com

Phone: +91-9357710014, +91-9465468291

INTRODUCTION

Firstly, I humbly offer my respectful obeisances to all peoples of the world. I feel particularly happy to present this book which should signify of our commitment. The pace of life is so rapid these days that most of the times we cannot even remember that we are very imperfect mortal human beings living in a material transient world. In this a tool for promoting the path to peace is devotional service. The purpose of writing this book is to systematically propagate spiritual knowledge to society at large and to enlighten all the peoples in the approach of spiritual life in order to check the imbalance of values in life and to achieve real unity and peace as well as to extend love for this cosmic life beings such as aquatics, plants, insects, birds, animals, human kinds etc. So, my research is to further understand the world peaceful by laws of God (scriptures) and to how this knowledge can be applied to better everyday life. It is an integral part of problem solving. Lastly, I do wish this book will a very auspicious for each knowledge giver to spread the positive message across the world without any boundaries and bring joy and wisdom to readers' lives peacefully.

Author

A. Debachandra Singh

THE MATCHLESS GIFT FOR UNIVERSAL PEACEFUL LIFE

CONTENTS

(A) THE CONCEPTS OF GOD

(1) *Vedic Concept of God*

* In Vedic Literature, there exist two different concepts : God (Bhagavan) and Demigod (Devata). Lord Shri Krishna is the source of all demigods who assist Him in various worldly affairs. There are 33 crores (330 millions) of demigods _ each one of them works under Lord Shri Krishna's direction. Krishna, the meaning of the word in Sanskrit is all - attractive. From practical experience we can observe that one is attractive due to (1) wealth, (2) power, (3) fame, (4) beauty, (5) wisdom and (6) renunciation. One who is in possession of all six of these opulences at the same time and who possesses them to an unlimited degree is understood to be the Supreme Personality of Godhead according to Parasara Muni a great Vedic authority. Krishna naturally has his own personal identity, just a each of us does. Personhood is not a limited concept when applied to God, or the Absolute Truth. The Vedas (scriptures of ancient India) define Krishna as the supreme conscious being among all other conscious beings. He is infinite, we are finite. He is unlimited responsible for the creation, maintenance and annihilation of everything in the material world. Any descriptions of the Supreme Being may seem incredible unless we consider that the ultimate source of everything, the Absolute Truth, the Supreme Person, God is also the origin of all the forms. Our forms in the material world are temporary, changeable and often causes of misery but the Absolute Truth is eternal, unchanging and blissful.

(2) *Islamic Concept of God*

* Muslims often refer to God as Allah. This is a universal name of God and does not refer to an exclusively 'Islamic' God. God is the Creator and the Sustainer of the universe who created everything for a reason. Muslims believe that He created humankind with a simple purpose to worship Him. He sent messengers to guide in fulfilling this

purpose. Some of these messengers include Adam, Noah, Abraham, Moses, Jesus and Muhammad, peace be upon all of them. They all taught a consistent message about God by affirming His greatness as the Creator and guiding people to worship Him alone.

(3) *God - Concept of Christianity*

* In Christianity, God is the eternal being who created and preserves all the things. Christians believe God to be both transcendent and immanent. Christian teachings of the immanence and involvement of God and His love for humanity exclude the belief that God is of same substance as the created universe but accept that God's divine nature was hypostatically united to human nature the person of Jesus Christ, in an event known as the Incarnation. God is further held to have the properties of Holiness, Justice, Omnibenebolence and Omnipresence. Christians believe all we know about God is through God showing or revealing himself to people and this process is known as 'revelation' .

(4) *God - Concept of Judaism*

* In Judaism, God has been conceived in a variety of ways. Traditionally, Judaism holds that Yahweh, the God of Abraham, Issac and Jacob and the national of the Israelites, delivered the Israelites from slavery in Egypt, and gave the Laws of Moses at biblical Mount Sinai as described in the Torah. According to the rationalist stream of Judaism articulated by Maimonides, which later came to dominate much of official traditional Jewish thought, God is understood as the absolute one, indivisible and incomparable being who is the ultimate cause of all existence. Traditional interpretations of Judaism generally emphasize that God is personal yet also transcendent, while some modern interpretations of Judaism emphasize that God is a force or ideal. The names of God used most often in the Hebrew Bible are the Tetragrammaton (YHWH Hebrew : n / n') and Elohim. Other names of God in traditional Judaism include EL Shaddai and Shekhinah.

(5) <u>God - Concept of Buddhism</u>

* Buddhism is a philosophy which does not include the belief in a creation deity, or any eternal divine personal being. It teaches that there are divine beings or gods, heavens and rebirths in its doctrine of cyclical rebirth, but it considers none of these gods as a creator or as being eternal. In Buddhism there is no belief in a personal God. Buddhists believe that nothing is fixed or permanent and that change is always possible. The path to Enlightenment is through the practice and development of morality, meditation and wisdom. But for an earnest believer, the God - idea is more than a mere device for explaining external facts like the origin of the world. For him it is an object of faith that can bestow a strong feeling of certainty, not only as to God's existence "somewhere out there," but as to God's consoling presence and closeness to himself.

REFERENCE

1. Some Related Religious Texts
2. God In Judaism – Wikipedia

(B) CREATION AND LAWS OF NATURE

Creation: The Creation, the original bringing into existence of the universe by God.

(I) <u>Creation according to Islam</u>

* Now we come to the concept on this topic. The Quran offers insights into the phenomenon of the creation of the universe and prescribes with great clarity that God created everything as the following verse of the Quran stages :

"Such is Allah; your Lord, There is no God but He the Creator of all things, so worship Him. And He is guardian over everything."

According to the foregoing Quranic verse, everything is the creation of God. The following two verses of the Quran and the Arabic word used in them sheds further light on this topic :

"The Originator of heavens and the earth ! How can He have a son when He has no consort and when He has created everything and has knowledge of all things ?"

"He is the Originator of the heavens and the earth. When He decrees a thing. He only says to it 'Be' and it is."

Therefore, as the aforementioned verses of the Quran's clearly reveal the creation of the universe was not a spontaneous phenomenon Allah created everything. According to Quran, His decree can create anything out of nothing. And since God created everything it follows that no entity shares eternity with the Creator. To examine the true meaning of these verses we shall render an etymological of the Arabic word "Badi" used therein.

The word "Badi" is often translated as the "Originator," which is one of the names and attributes of God used in the Quran. The dictionary of Lane translates "Badi" as (He) the originator of creation, according to His own will, not after the similitude of anything pre - existing. "However, historically "Badi" has been used in a more wide – ranging fashion and its use is not restricted to connoting "Originator." Old dictionaries such as the "Al - Mufradat fi Gharib al - Quran" by Allama Raghib Isphahani, compiled almost nine hundred years ago, explains that "Badi" when used in connection with God signifies, "originating the creation of a thing without any tool, matter, time or place," Keeping these meanings ascribed to the word "Badi" in mind, we can submit conclusively that the Quran credits the entire process of the creation of the universe to God and provides that at the time of creation, matter and space did not exist even time was the creation of Allah.

* The Quran says that "the heavens and the earth were joined together as one unit, before We clove them asunder" (21 : 30). Allah "turned to the sky, and it had been (as) smoke. He said to it and to the earth : Come together, willingly or unwillingly. 'They said : ' We come (together) in willing obedience" (42 : 11). Thus the elements and what was to become the planets and stars to cool, come together, and form into shape, following the natural laws that Allah established in the universe. The Quran further states that Allah created the sun, the moon, and the planets, each with their own individual courses or orbits. "It is He Who created the night and the day, and the sun and moon ; all (the celestial bodies) swim along, each in its rounded course" (21 : 33). "The heavens, We have built them with power. And verily, We have expanding it" (51 : 47). The Quran states that "Allah created the heavens and the earth, and all that is between them, in six days" (7 : 54). While on the surface this might seem similar to the account related in the Bible, there are some important distinctions. The verses that mention 'six days' use the Arabic word "youm" (day). This word appears several other times in the Quran, each denoting a different measurement of time. In one case, the measure of a day is equated with 50,000 years (70 : 4), whereas another verse states that "a day in the sight of your Lord is like 1,000 years of your reckoning" (22 : 47). The word "youm" is thus understood, within the Quran, to be a long period of time an era or eon. Therefore, Muslims interpret the description of a "six day" creation as six distinct periods or eons. The length of these periods

is not precisely defined, nor are the specific developments that took place during each period.

* After completing the Creation, the Quran describes that Allah "settled Himself upon the Throne" (57 : 4) to oversee His work. A distinct point is made to counter the Biblical idea of a day of rest : "We created the heavens and the earth and all that is between them in six days, nor did any sense of wearing touch Us" (50 : 38). Allah is never done with His work, because the process of creation is ongoing. Each new child who is born, every seed that sprouts into a sapling, every new species that appears on earth, is part of the ongoing process of Allah's creation. "He it is Who created the heavens and the earth in six days, then established Himself on the Throne. He knows what enters within the heart of the earth, and what comes forth out of it, what comes down from heaven, and what mounts up to it. And He is with you wherever you may be. And Allah sees well all that you do" (57 : 4). The Quranic account of creation is in line with modern scientific thought about the development of the universe and life on earth. Muslims acknowledge that life developed over a long period of time, but see Allah's power behind it all. Descriptions of creation in the Quran are set in context to remind the readers of Allah's majesty and wisdom. "What is the matter with you, that you are not conscious of Allah's majesty, seeing that it is He who has created you in diverse stages? See you not how Allah has created the seven heavens one above another, and made the moon a light in their midst, and made the sun as a (glorious) lamp? And Allah has produced you from the earth, growing (gradually)" (71 : 13 : 17).

* The Quran describes that Allah "made from water every living thing" (21 : 30). Another verse describes how "Allah has created every animal from water. Of them are some that creep on their bellies, some that walk on two legs, and some that walk on four. Allah creates what He wills, for truly Allah has power over all things" (24 : 45). These verses support the scientific theory that life began in the Earth's oceans. While Islam recognizes the general idea of the development of life in stages, over a period of time, human

beings are considered as a special act of creation. Islam teaches that human beings are a unique life form that was created by Allah in a special way, with unique gifts and abilities unlike any other: a soul and conscience, knowledge, and free will. In short, Muslims do not believe that human beings randomly evolved from apes. The life of human beings began with the creation of two people, a male and a female named Adam and Hawwa (Eve). The Quran describes how Allah created Adam : "We created man from sounding clay, from mud moulded into shape........" (15 : 26). And, "He began the creation of man from clay, and made his progeny from a quintessence of fluid" (32:7:8). Thus, human beings have a fundamental attachment to the earth. While the creation of Eve is not described in detail, the Quran does make it clear a 'mate' was created with Adam from the same nature and soul. "It is He who created you from a single person, and made his mate of like nature, in order that he might dwell with her in love" (7 : 189). She is not mentioned by name in the Quran, but in Islamic tradition she is known as Hawwa (Eve). From these two individuals, generations of human beings have inhabited the earth. "Oh human kind! We created you from a single pair of a male and a female, and made you into nations and tribes, so that you may know each other (not that ye may despite each other). Verily the most honoured among you in the sight of Allah is the who is the most righteous of you. And Allah has full knowledge and is well acquainted (with all things)" (49: 13).

(2) The Creation of Heaven and Earth
according to the Bible as called Genesis

(i) In the beginning God created the heaven and the earth. And the earth was without form and void ; and darkness was upon the face of the deep. And the Spirit of God was hovering upon face of the waters. And God said, Let there be light ; and there was light. And God saw the light, that it was good ; and God divided light from the darkness. And God called the light Day, and the darkness he called Night. And the evening and the morning were the First Day.

(ii) Then God said, Let there be a firmament in the midst of the waters, and let it divide the water from waters. And God made the firmament, and divided the waters which were under the firmament from the waters which were above the firmament : and it was so. And God called the firmament Heaven. And the evening and the morning were the Second Day.

(iii) Then God said, Let the waters under the heaven be gathered together unto one place, and let the dry land appear : and it was so. And God called the dry land Earth ; and the gathering together of the waters called the Seas : and God saw that it was good. And God said, Let the earth bring forth grass, the herb yielding seed, and the fruit tree yielding fruit after his kind, whose seed is in itself, upon the earth : and it was so. And the earth brought forth grass, and herb yielding seed after his kind, the tree yielding fruit, whose seed was in itself, after his kind : and God saw that it was good. And the evening and the morning were the Third Day.

(iv) Then God said, Let there be lights in the firmament of the heaven to divide the day from the night ; and let them be for signs, and for seasons, and for days and years. And let them be for lights in the firmament of the heaven to give light upon the earth : and it was so. And God made two great lights ; the greater light to rule the day, and the lesser light to rule the night : He made stars also. And God set them in the firmament of the heaven to give light upon the earth, And to rule over the day and over the night, and to divide the light from the darkness : and God saw that it was good. And the evening and the morning were the Fourth Day.

(v) Then God said, Let the waters bring forth abundantly the moving creature that hath life, and fowl that may fly above the earth in the open firmament of heaven. And God created great whales, and every living creatures that moveth, which the waters brought forth abundantly, after their kind, and every winged fowl after His kind : and God saw that was good. And God blessed them, saying, Be fruitful, and multiply, and fill the water in the seas, and let fowl multiply in the earth. And the evening and the morning were the Fifth Day.

(vi) Then God said, Let the earth bring forth the living creatures after their kind, cattle, and creeping things, and the beast of the earth after their kind : and it was so. And God made the beast of the earth after their kind, and cattle after their kind, and everything that creepeth upon the earth after their kind : and God saw that it was good. And God said, Let us make man in our image, after you likeness : and let them have dominion over the fish of the sea, and over the fowl of the air, and over the cattle, and over all the earth, and over every creeping thing that creepeth upon the earth. So God created man in His own image, in the image of God created He him ; man and female created He then. And God blessed them, and God said unto them, Be fruitful, and multiply, and replenish the earth, and subdue it : and have dominion over the fish of the sea, and over the fowl of the air, and over every living thing the moveth upon the earth. And God said, Behold, I have given you every herb bearing seed, which is upon the face of all the earth, and every tree, in the which is the fruit of a tree yielding seed ; to you it shall be for food. And to every beast of the earth, and to every fowl of the air, and to everything that creepeth upon the earth, wherein there is life, I have given every green herb for food : and it was so. And God saw everything that He had made, and, behold, it was very good. And the evening and the morning were the Sixth Day.

(vii) Thus the heavens and the earth were finished, and all the host of them And on the Seventh Day, God ended His work which He had made : and He rested on the Seventh Day from all His work which He had made. And God blessed the Seventh Day, and sanctified it : because that in it He had rested from all his work which created and made.

(3) Creation According to Vedic Scriptures

(i) What was there before Creation ?

*   Supreme personality of God head, Lord Shri Krishna who is beyond material creation exists before creation and after annihilation. Period after annihilation and before creation all living entities are dormant in the form of Lord. Where there is vibration there is a sound. Conversely, to produce a sound the vibration corresponding to it must also be created. The scientific concept that the different vibrations of the same energy are the cause of creation is the same as the belief that world was created with the breath of the Paramatma (Supreme Self) manifesting itself as the sound of the Vedas.

(ii) Root of Creation

The false - ego of the jiva (an individual soul) is the root cause of creation. Every jiva has a minute independence to take decisions either to utilize in the service of the Lord or to lord it over.

(iii) Purpose of Creation

(1)   To Reclaim the condition souls who are dormant in forgetfulness --- heart of Krishna (Shrimad Bhagavatam 3. 5. 3 and 3. 5. 24)

(2)   Lord wants to enjoy with creation of material world (S B 3. 5. 22 p)

(3)   He wants all parts and parcel to participate in raslila---the highest living condition (S B 3. 5. 23 p)

(4)   Chance for the jiva to enjoy sense gratification and to realize that they are created for transcendental sense (S B 3. 5. 51)

(5)   The purpose of the universal creation is to realize the goals set forth by God and to reach god (S B 7. 5. 31)

Process of Creation

(1) Lord Krishna is the cause of all causes and from His various expansions, Maha - Vishnu appears, accompanied by all the ingredients of material creation. From His body pores millions of universes of various sizes and properties come out with every exhalation.

(2) Maha - Vishnu glances over material nature, which is eternal and by His specific functional expansion, Sambhu (Shiva), injects the living entities (souls) into material nature. The living entities are eternal and fragmental parts of Lord Krishna

(3) Maha - Vishnu expands as Garbhodaksayi - Vishnu and enters into each universe.

(4) Garbhodaksayi - Vishnu creates the Vedas and enters into the atomic particles (atoms) as Ksirodaksayi - Vishnu ,who enters into the heart of all living beings as Paramatma, the super soul.

(5) A lotus flower sprouts from the naval of Garbhodaksayi-Vishnu, and the first living being in the universe, Lord Brahma, appears from it.

(6) Ksirodaksayi - Vishnu from within the heart of Lord Brahma imparts Vedic knowledge, which he uses to create everything within the universe : the planets, plants, animals, humans, demigods and rishis (holy sages).

(7) From the forehead of Lord Brahma, Lord Shiva appears, who is an expansion of Sadashiva (Lord Shiva in the spiritual world). Lord Shiva plays a role in the creation of living beings and destruction, and is known as Rudra in this role.

(8) After 311.040 Trillion years, Lord Shiva destroys everything within the universe and the empty shell of the universe goes back into the body pore of Maha - Vishnu. Who now inhales and all the universes go back into His body pores.

(9) Dull matter or a bang (big or small) or an invisible force cannot create anything. It's the power of the Supreme Person, Lord

Krishna that creates and maintains millions of universes. The unlimited opulences of Lord Krishna are completely beyond our material conception.

"The whole cosmic order is under Me. Under My will it is automatically manisfested again and again, and under My will it is annihilated at the end." (Lord Krishna, BG 9.8).

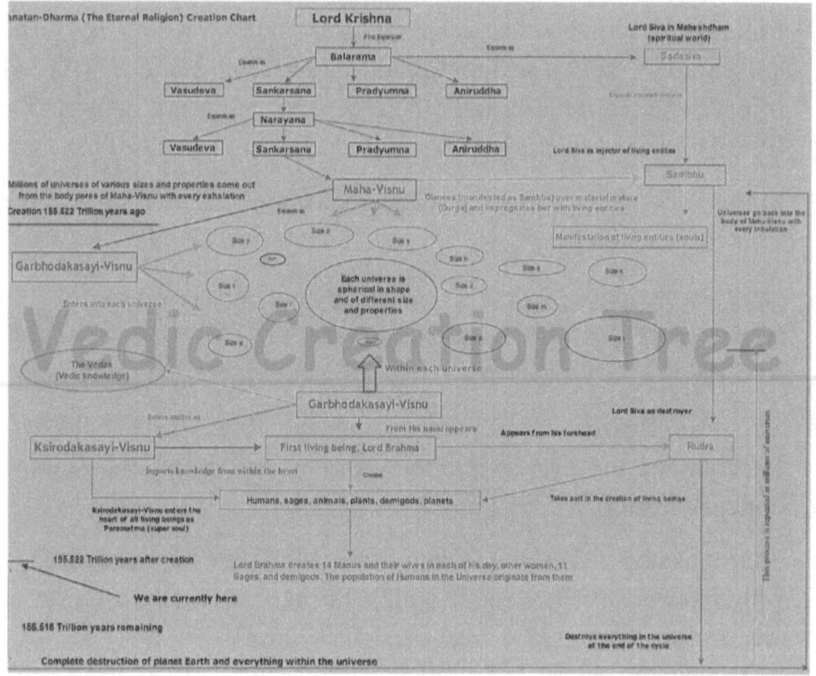

Creation Chart

(4) Laws of Nature

*   Laws of nature means laws of God. There is no difference between laws of nature and laws of God. Therefore Bhagavata says that religious principle cannot be manufactured by any human being. It is the law of God. There one has to obey. One cannot disobey. It will be enforce upon us. Just like law of nature, the winter season. We cannot change it. It will be enforced upon us. Law of nature, summer season, we cannot change it anything. Laws of nature or laws of God, the sun is rising from the eastern side and setting on the western side. We cannot change it. The universe around us appears to be orderly and symmetrical. The planets rotate perfectly in their orbits. Our bodies possess complex circulatory, respiratory, and digestive systems. Even the atoms are highly structured. That we have to understand, how laws of nature is going on. That is process of God, to understand laws of nature. And as soon as speak of laws of nature, we must accept that there is a lawmaker. Laws of nature cannot develop automatically. There must be some authority on the background. Bhagavat gita therefore says in the Tenth Chapter that "Under My direction, superintendence, the material laws are working." (BG 9 -- 10). In Vedic literature, it is said, Dharma, religion, means the codes given by God, and we have to abide by those laws. When we do not abide by those laws, then we violate the laws of nature, of God, and we become punishable.

(5) Relationship between Man and Nature

*   The ancient view of nature has been dominated by the religious concept that nature is a product of God and one should respect nature and its variegated manifestations. However, with the advent of scientific revolution from around the sixteenth century, man's thinking about nature has changed significantly. Science has practically replaced religion as pre - eminent intellectual authority about the world view of nature. In this view the mechanical concept of the universe and of nature became increasingly influential. The discovery of the gravitational law, the laws of physics and chemistry,

the laws of mechanics___classical as well as quantum___and the laws of genetics, conceiving the big bang theories of the origin of universe, life and so on are all attempts to find a deeper grasp of the hidden principles of nature. The scientific mind (materialism) makes two prime assertions (1) the scientific process is the only reliable means to knowledge (2) matter is the fundamental reality of nature. The first is an epistemological assertion; the second is an ontological assertion about the reality of nature. Rationalism and empiricism have become the two bases of modern epistemology. The validity of these assertions on an historical perspective ancient, modern and postmodern and will make some observations in the light of the current global developments in the search for meaning about the relationship between man and nature.

REFERENCES

1. Islam Creation Story
2. The Creation Story in brief, as found in The Holy Quran
3. Holy Bible Genesis
4. Vedic Creation Chart Iskcon Inc.

(C) THE IMPACT OF RELIGIOUS ASPECTS ON GLOBALIZATION

*   Religion is that which connects us with God. If it is not capable of connecting us with God, it is not religion. Religion means searching for God, understanding God and establishing a relationship with God. This is religion. In the present day most people claim to be devoted to some religions Christian, Hindu, Muslim, Buddhist, etc. but in fact they do not really believe in the scriptures. Those who do believe in the scriptures are, by and large attached to pious philanthropic activities. They believe that religion means yajna (sacrifice), dana (charity) and tapas (penance). "Religion means the codes of God." The codes of religion are like state laws. The state gives us rules and regulations to live by, and one who follows the rules and regulations or laws, of the state is called a good citizen. Those who do not follow are called outlaws or rogues. Similarly, religion is a simple thing : to accept the orders of God. That's all. It doesn't matter what religion you follow. You may be a Christian, I may be Hindu, someone may be a Muhammadan, but the test of religion is how one has developed his/her God consciousness.

Some Religious Aspects of Globalization :

(1) Sanamahism

*   The Meetei or Meitei of Kangleipak (Manipur) started to worship objects and later regarded Sanamahi (spreading like liquid everywhere) the son of Tengbanba Mapu as their supreme deity. Sanamahi religion is one of the oldest religious of South - East Asia. It originated in Manipur state north - eastern part of India and mainly worshipped by the Meiteis, Kabui and Zeliangrong few other communities who inhabit in Manipur, Assam, Tripura, U. P., Myanmar, Bangladesh, etc. Along with Sanamahi, in the past, religious space within Meitei homes called Sanamahi Kachin were dedicated to Leimarel Sidabi and Phungga. This is also in modern Meitei

families who identify with Sanamahism, and the followers as Sanamahist. The holy scripture of Sanamahism is called "Sanamahi - Puya."

(2) Jainism

* Jainism is an ancient religion from India that reaches way to liberation by living the lives of harmlessness and renunciation. The essence of Jainism is concern for the welfare of every being in the universe and for the health of universe itself. Jains are strict vegetarians and live in a way that minimises their use of world's resources. There are 24 tirthankaras as per Jain beliefs. The first tirthankaras was Rishabh dev Or Adinath. The last tirthankar was Mahavir and also the founder of Jainism. Jainism believe that human beings as well as animal and plants contain living souls. Each of these souls is considered of equal value and should be treated with respect and compassion. The three guiding principles of Jainism are (1) Right Vision (2) Right Knowledge and (3) Right Conduct. The supreme principle of Jainism is non - violence (Ahimsa).

(3) Zoroastrianism

* Zoroastrianism is one of the world's oldest monotheistic religions. It was founded by Persian Prophet Zoroaster in ancient Iran approximately 3500 years ago. Zoroastrians believe that there is only one God called Ahura Mazda (Wise Lord) and he created the world. Ahura Mazda revealed the truth and teachings through Zoroaster. Zoroastrians pray several times a day. The holy scripture of Zoroastrians is called Avesta. Zoroastrian teachings and practices in the Arabic - speaking world.

(4) Taoism

* Taoism is an ancient tradition of philosophy and religious belief that is deeply rooted in Chinese customs. Taoism is also as Daoism which is more accurate as per Chinese accent. Its literal meaning is the way. It is the religion of unity and opposites : Yin and Yang. The principle of Yin and Yang sees the world as filled with complementary forces action and non - action, light and dark, hot and cold and so on. In Taoism, the purpose of life is inner peace and harmony. The founder of the religion is generally recognized to be man named Laozi, who lived sometime in the

sixth century C. E. in China. Taoist beliefs emphasize the virtues of compassion and moderation.

(5) Sikhism

* Sikhism was founded by Guru Nanak in 15th century in northern parts of India specially present Punjab region. The most important part in Sikhism is the internal religious state of the individual. It stresses the importance of doing good actions rather than merely carrying out rituals. The Sikh scripture is Guru Granth Sahib, a book that Sikhs consider a living guru. Sikhs believe that the way to lead a good life is to God in heart and mind at all times, live honestly and work hard, treat everyone equally, be generous to the less fortunate, serve others.

(6) Shintoism

* Shintoism is a direct descendant of the animistic folk religion of the Yayoi, whose culture spread from the north of Kyushu to the rest of Japan from 3rd century C. E. onward. The primary focus of Shinto is the nature belief in Kami (spirits) and interaction with them through public shrines. These shrines are an essential artificial of and for Shinto observation. Traditional Japanese styles of dress, dance, and ritual are also rooted in Shinto customs. Shinto is unique among religions. As a reflection of Japanese identity. Shinto observance is not necessarily to those who view themselves as religious adherents.

(7) Buddhism

* Buddhism is the world's fourth - largest religion with over 520 million followers, or over 7 % of the global population, known as Buddhists. Its practice has historically been most prominent in East and Southeast Asia, but its influence is growing in the West. Many Buddhist ideas and philosophies overlap with those of other faiths, Followers of Buddhism don't acknowledge a supreme god or deity. They instead focus on achieving enlightenment - a state of inner peace and wisdom. When followers reach this spiritual echelon, they are said to have experienced nirvan. The religion's, Buddha, is considered an extraordinary man, but not a god. The word Buddha means "enlightened." Buddhism encourages

its people to avoid self - indulgence but also self - denial. Buddha's most important teachings, known as The Four Noble Truths are essential to understanding the religion. Buddhists embrace the concepts of Karma (the law of cause and effect) and reincarnation (the continuous cycle of rebirth). Followers of Buddhism can worship in temples or in their own homes. Buddhist monks follow a strict code of conduct, which includes celibacy. There is no single Buddhist symbol, but a number of images have evolved that represent Buddhist beliefs, including the lotus flower, the eight - spoke dharma wheel, the Bodhi tree, etc.

(8) Judaism

*   Judaism is the world's oldest monotheistic religion, dating back nearly 4,000 years. Followers of Judaism believe in one God who revealed himself through ancient prophet. The history of Judaism is essential to understanding the Jewish faith, which has a rich heritage of Law, culture and tradition. Jewish people believe there is only one God who has established a covenant or special agreement with them. Their God communicates to believers through prophets and rewards good deeds while also punishing evil. Most Jews (with the exception of a few groups) believe that their Messiah has not yet come but will one day. Jewish people worship in holy places known as synagogue, and their spiritual leaders are called rabbis. The six - pointed Star of David is the symbol of Judaism. Today, there are about 14 million Jews worldwide. Most of them live in the United States and Israel. Traditionally, a person is considered Jewish if his or her mother is Jewish. The Jewish sacred text is called the Tanakh or the "Hebrew Bible." It includes the book as the old Testament. According to Hebrew man named Abraham, who became known as the founder of Judaism.

(9) Christianity

*   billion adherents, or 33% of the total population. Christianity is monotheistic, deontological, grass - roots, Jewish sectarian movement that focus upon the life, teachings and mission of the Jesus of Nazareth (also known as Jesus the Christ). It began in Jerusalem in Judea in the 1st century C. E., and moved northward in the Mediterranean region through the efforts and activities of Jesus's personally chosen disciples and

apostles. Christian believe there is only one God, he created the heavens and the earth. This divine Godhead consists of three parts : the father (God himself), the son (Jesus Christ) and the holy Spirit. The essence of Christianity revolves around the life, death, and Christian beliefs on the resurrection of Jesus. Christians believe God sent his son Jesus, the Messiah, to save the world. They believe Jesus was crucified on a cross to offer the forgiveness of sins and was resurrected three days after his death before ascending to heaven. The Holy Bible includes important scriptures that outline Jesus's teachings, the lives and teachings of major prophets and offer instructions for how Christians should live. Both Christians and Jews follow the Old Testament of the Bible, but Christians also embrace the New Testament. The cross is symbol of Christianity. The Churches are places where Christians worship. The most important Christian holidays are Christmas (which celebrates the birth of Jesus) and Easter (which commemorates the resurrection of Jesus).

(10) Islamism

* Islam is the second largest religion in the world after Christianity, with about 1•8 billion Muslims worldwide. Although its roots go back further, scholars typically date the creation of Islam to the 7th century, making it the youngest of the major world religions. Islam started in Mecca, in modern - day Saudi Arabia, during the time of the prophet Muhammad's life. Today the faith is spreading rapidly throughout the world. The word "Islam" means "submission to the will of God." Followers of Islam are called Muslims. Muslims are monotheistic and worship one, all - knowing God, who in Arabic is known as Allah. Followers of Islam aim to live a life of complete submission to Allah. They believe that nothing can happen without Allah's permission, but human have free will. Islam teaches that Allah's word was revealed to the prophet Muhammad through the angel Gabriel some time around 600 B. C. E.. Mosques are places where Muslims worship. Some important Islamic holy places include the Kaaba shrine in Mecca, the Al - Aqsa mosque in Jerusalem, and the Prophet Muhammad's mosque in Medina. The Quran is the major holy text of Islam. The Hadith is another important book. Followers worship Allah by praying and reciting the Quran. They believe there will be a day of judgement and life after death. A central idea in Islam is jihad "which means" struggle. "While the term has been used

negatively in mainstream culture. Muslims believe it refers to internal and external effort to defend their faith."

(11) Candomble' Religion

*   Candomble is an African - Brazilian religion. It was born of a people who were taken from their homes in Africa and transplanted to Brazil during the slave trade. The religion is a mixture of traditional Yoruba, Fon and Bantu beliefs which originated from different regions in Africa, and it has also incorporated some aspects of the Catholic faith over time. The name itself means 'dance in honour of the gods', and music and dance are important parts of Candomble ceremonies. Practitioners of Candomble 'Religion believe in our powerful God called Oludumare' who is served by lesser deities. These deities are called Orixas. Candomble believe that each person has their own Orixa. These Orixa controls their destiny and protects them. Worship takes place in temples which have indoor and outdoor spaces as well as special spaces for the gods. Prior to entering, worshippers must wear clean clothes and ritually wash.

(12) Confucianism

*   Confucianism was a dominant form of philosophy and religious orientation in ancient China, one that emerged from the teachings of Chinese philosopher Confucius, who lived 551 --- 479 B.C.E.. Confucius viewed himself as a channel for the theological ideas emerging from the imperial dynasties that came before him. With an emphasis on family and social harmony, Confucianism was a distinctly humanist and even secularist religious ideology. Confucianism had a profound impact on the development of Eastern legal customs and the emergence of a scholar class. Confucianism would engage in a historic push and pull with the philosophies of Buddhism and Taoism, experiencing ebbs and flows influence, with high points during the Han, Tang and Song Dynasties. Confucianism does provide for a supernatural worldview (it incorporates Heaven, the Lord on High and divination) influenced by Chinese folk tradition.

(13) Yazidism / Yasdanism

* Yazidism (Cult of Angels) is a syncretic, monotheistic religion practiced by the Yazidis, an ethnoreligious group which resides primarily in northern Iraq, northern Syria and Southern Turkey. Yazidism incorporated elements of Zoroastrianism, Manichaeism, Gnosticism, Christianity and Islamism, all of which coalesced from 1162 C. E. to the 15th century C. E.. Ultimately this process created Yazidi culture and ethnic identity. They reconcile the existence of Abrahamic prophets with a doctrine of reincarnation and the belief that world is defended from evil by seven 'angels.' The Chief divine being is Malak Taus, who is worshipped in form of a peacock. The Yazidi religious centre and object of the annual pilgrimage is the tomb of Sheikh Adi, in the town of Lalish, Iraq. Two short books, Book of Revelation and Black Book, form the sacred scriptures of the Yazidis. They pray facing the sun at sun - rise, noon, and sunset. Wednesday is their holiday and Saturday is their the day of rest. Marriage outside the community is forbidden. A variety of foods are forbidden as is blue clothing. Yazidis believe in the existence of one God named Xwede. He is benevolent, all - forgiving and merciful deity, as well as the creation of the universe.

(14) Druzism

* Druze refer to an Arabic ethnoreligious group that originated in and still largely inhabits the Mountain of Druze region in southern Syria. Despite a small population of adherents, the Druze nonetheless play an important role in the development of their region (known in historical shorthand as the Levant). The Druze view themselves as the direct descendants of Jethro of Midian, distinguished in Jewish scriptures as the father - in - law of Moses. The Druze consider Jethro a "hidden" prophet, one through whom God spoke to "revealed prophet" Moses. As such, the Druze are considered related to Judaism by marriage. Like their in - laws, the Druze are monotheistic, professing faith in only one God. Druze ideologies are incorporating the wisdom of Greek philosophers, such as Plato and even though the culture originally developed out of Islamism, Druze do not identify as Muslim. Druze believe that at the end of rebirth

which is achieved through successive reincarnations, the soul is united with Cosmic Mind. They call themselves Unitarians (muwahhidun).

(15) Baha'i

*   Baha'i is the youngest major religion, founded in 1863 by the prophet Baha' 'u' lla'h. Baha'i grew out of the earlier religion of Babism, whose founder the Bab presaged the coming of another great prophet like the coming of Muhammad. Baha'i originated in Iran, although its current center is in Haifa, Israel Baha'i is a monotheistic religion, but it teaches that religious truth is manifested and revealed by the founders of all the major world religions, including Jesus Christ and the Buddha. Baha'i is believed that the same goal, and they strive for prosperity across faiths. Thus Baha'i has three principle teachings Unity of religion and Unity of humanity.

(16) Rastafarianism

*   Rastafari is a young Africa centered religion which developed in Jamaica in 1930s. This religion came to existence after the coronation of Haile Selassie as the King of Ethiopia in 1930. Followness of Rastafari are known as Rastafarians, Rastas, Suffers, Dreads or Dreadlocks. They believe that Haile Selassie is God and that he will return to Africa to rescue the black community who are living in exile due to colonisation and slave trade. Selassie was viewed by Rastafari as the Second Coming, a direct descendant of Christ, the Messiah foretold in the Book of Revelation.

(17) Hinduism

*   Hinduism is the oldest religion in the world, originating in Central Asia and the Indus Valley, still practiced in the present day. The term Hinduism is what is known as an exonym (a name given by others to a people, place, or concept) and derives from the Persian term Sindhus designating those who lived across the Indus River. Thus, the word "Hindu" originates from the Sanskrit word for river, Sindhu. Today, with about 900 million followers, Hinduism is the third - largest religion behind Christianity and Islamism. Roughly 95% of the world's Hindus live in India. Because the religion has no specific founded, it is difficult

to trace its origins and history. Hinduism is unique in that it is not a single religion but a compilation of many traditions and philosophers. Hindus believe in the doctrine of samsara (the continuous cycle of life, death and reincarnation) and karma (the universal law of cause and effect). One of the key thoughts of Hinduism is "Atma" or the belief in soul. This philosophy holds that living creatures have a soul and they are all parts of the supreme soul. The goal is to achieve "moksha" or salvation which ends the cycle of rebirths to become part of the absolute truth. Hindu revere all living creatures and considered the cow a sacred animal. Most of Hindu don't eat beef or pork, and many are vegetarians. Hinduism is closely related to other Indian religions, including Buddhism, Sikhism and Jainism, etc. The primary sacred texts, known as the Vedas, were composed around 1500 B.C.. This collection of verses and hymns was written in Sanskrit and contains revelations received by ancient saints and sages. Hindu worship many gods and goddesses in addition to Brahman (atma Or soul), name as (1) Brahma (the god responsible for the creation of the world and all living things) (2) Vishnu (the god that preserves and protects the universe) (3) Shiva (the god that destroys the universe in order to recreate it) (4) Devi (the goddess that fights to restore dharma (5) Krishna (the god of compassion, tenderness and love) (6) Lakshmi (the goddess of wealth and purity) (7) Saraswati (the goddess of learning) (8) Ganesh (the god of intellect and wisdom), etc. One may worship the Divine at one's home, a personal shrine, or a temple. Hindu temples are adorned with figures of many gods both inside and externally. The statue is thought to embody the deity itself and one receives blessings and comfort through eye contact.

REFERENCES

1. Related Religious Texts
2. Religious Topics found in Websites

(D) INCARNATIONS OF LORD SHRI KRISHNA

* The Lord Vishnu as incarnation and the Supreme Lord Shri Krishna as source, in His various forms, decends from the spiritual sky to the material universe with a particular mission. In the Vedic Scriptures, it is mentioned that whenever evil triumphs over good, or whenever darkness takes over the light (truth), or unjust rules over justice, then Lord Krishna will take birth on earth in order to restore Dharma (righteous). The incarnations that Lord Krishna takes are called avatars.There are six kinds of incarnations of Lord Shri Krishna : (1) the purasa - avatar (2) the lila - avatar (3) the guna - avatar (4) the manvantara - avatar (5) the yuga- avatar and (6) the saktyavesa - avatar. Even though there are innumerable incarnations of the Lord Krishna, some of the important ones are mentioned in Srimad Bhagavatam Canto 1 Chapter 3. together, Lord has reincarnated 23 times and every time, he's taken a different form. It is predicted that He will appear one last time at the end of Kaliyuga, making the number 24.

*   Here is the complete list of all those 24 avatars of Lord Krishna as they are : (1) Adi Purush (2) Four Kumars (3) Nara Narayan (5) Kapila (6) Dattatreya (7) Yajna (8) Rishabha (9) Prithu (10) Dhanavatati (11) Mohini (12) Hayagreeva (13) Vyasa (14) Matsya Avatar (15) Kurma Avatar (16) Varaha Avatar (17) Narasimha (18) Vamana (19) Parashurama (20) Rama (21) Balarama (22) Krishna (23) Buddha and (24) Kalki Avatar. Of all the Avatars, Sri Krishna alone is considered a Purana Avatar, a direct and complete representation of the Supreme Divine Himself. The Poet Jayadeva Goswami also wrote a beautiful song about Lord Krishna's ten most prominent incarnations, called 'Dashavatar' out of these 24 avatars as following :

(1) Matsya Avatar / Fish or water life (all life on this planet started under water)

* All glories to you, O Lord of the universe, who took the form of fish. When the sacred hymns of Vedas were lost in the waters of universe devastation, you swam like a boat that vast ocean to rescue them.

Thankfully, Lord Sri Krishna noticed the theft the demon Hayagriva who had stolen the Vedas, the book of knowledge needed for the regeneration of the world, while Lord Brahma, responsible for recreating the world, was asleep and Lord Krishna descended to Earth in the form of a small fish known as the Matsya Avatar, the First Incarnation of Lord Himself. The Matsya Avatar represents the half fish, a half- human form of Lord slaying the demon Hayagriva. According to a story in the "Matsya Puran," Matsya informs Manu, the leader of the humans, of the great flood, and the helps him save all the motile living beings, the Vedas, and the seeds of all plants to sustain life.

(2) Kurma Avatar / the tortoise (Amphibious like tortoise, half on the water and half on the land)

*   All glories to you, O Lord of the universe, who took the form of a tortoise. When the ocean of milk was churned you became the pivot beneath the churning rod of Mount Mandara leaving a beautiful impression on your back.

Kurma Avatar represents the half tortoise, half- man form of Lord. When the devas (demigods) and asuras (demons) were churning the ocean of milk in order to get amitra, the nectar of immortality, with serpent Vasuki as the rope and the mount Mandaras as the churning staff, the mountain starts to sink, the Lord took the form of a tortoise to bear the weight of the mountain. In the end the demigods, who were his devotes, got immortal nectar. The demons who had worked so hard, but who did not have the blessing of Lord, got only disappointment and poison.

(3) Varaha Avatar / The Boar (Among the mammals, one animal which is strong, strongly rooted in its body is wild boar)

*   All glories to you, O Lord of the universe, who took the form of a boar. When the earth fell into the ocean at the bottom of the universe you caught her on your tusk, where she looked like a spot on the moon.

Varaha Avatar represents the half boar avatar of Lord. Varaha fought a fierce battle with Hiranyaksha, to save Earth. Hiranyaksha, had drowned the Earth away from the universe. Lord (Varaha) scooped out Earth the ocean of negativity with his tusks and thus protected it from getting doomed. When the demon Hiranyaksha stole the earth (goddess Bhudevi) and hid her in the primordial waters. Lord appeared as Varaha to rescue her. The battle between Varaha and Hiranyaksha is believed to have lasted for a thousand years. Varaha finally slew the demon and retrieved the earth from the ocean, lifting it on His tusks, and restored Bhudevi to her place in the universe.

(4) Narasimha Avatar / Half- Man and Half-Lion (Half man and Half animal)

* All glories to you, O Lord of the universe, who took the form of a man-lion. As easily as crushing a wasp between your fingers, you tore apart the demon Hiranyakshapu with the poited nails of your bare hands, which are beautiful like the lotus flower.

The demon Hiranyakashipu obtained a boon from Brahma and he could not be killed or harmed by any means. Now arrogant in his security, Hiranyakashipu began to cause trouble both in heaven and on earth. However, his son Prahlada was devoted to Lord. One day, when the demon challenged Prahlada. Lord emerged in the form of a man-lion known as Narasimha to slay the demon.

(5) Vaman Avatar (A Dwafted Man)

* All glories to you, O Lord of the universe, who took the form of a brahman dwarf. By covering the world in three steps you deceived Bali and released the waters of the Ganges, which flow from your toes to purify all beings of the world.

In Treta Yuga, Lord incarnated himself as Brahmin (Vamana) to end the role of the generous demon-king, Bali. The demon-king had forcefully captured three different worlds. When Lord, a Brahmin asked for three paces of land as measured by His own steps. Bali agreed to give away his head after he realised that it was Lord. He was granted moksha (salvation) after stepped over Bali's head.

(6) Parasurama Avatar / Warrior (A Full grown man but emotionally volatile man)

*   All glories to you, O Lord of the universe, who took the form of Parshuram. You battle the earth with the blood of the warriors whom you killed and washed away the sins of the world, releasing people from the free of material life.

Lord Parasurama is a Kshatriya. He is depicted as a sage with an axe in his hand. He was born to end the tyranny of the evil Kshatriyas, who misused their powers and made other's lives miserable and bring them to justice for the sake of humankind.

(7) Rama Avatar (Civilized and peaceful man)

* All glories to you, O Lord of the universe, who took the form of Rama. You distributed the ten heads of the terrible demon Ravana for the pleasure of the gods of the ten directions, fulfilling their desires to see him dead.

The prince and king of Ayodhya, Rama's life and journey is one of adherence to dharma (Righteous) despite harsh tests and obstacles and many pains of life and time. He is pictured as the ideal man and the perfect human. For the sake of his father's honour. Rama abandons his claim to Ayodhya's throne to serve an exile of fourteen years in the forest. While in exile from his own kingdom with his brother Lakshman and the monkey king Hanuman, his wife Sita was abducted by the demon king of Lanka, Ravana. He travelled to Ashoka Vatika in Lanka, killed the demon king and saved Sita.

(8) Balarama Avatar (The Cowherd)

* All glories to you, O Lord of the universe, who took the form of Balarama, carrying a plough. The garments on your brilliant white body are the colour of the Yamuna River - whose dark waters reflect the fresh rain clouds, and who was afraid of the striking of your plough.

When Lord Krishna came down to his world he did not come alone. With him were his eternal associates from the spiritual realm. Chief among them is his brother Balarama. Balarama is the direct expansion of Krishna, like a second candle lit from the first, of equal power and illumination. In this prayer from Gita-Govinda he is counted as the eight reincarnation of Lord. Like Rama, Balarama and Krishna lived in the forest as cowherds with their friends, the boys and girls of Vrindavan, the cows, the monkeys, the peacocks and the deers. Balarama always carried a plough, and he is particularly associated with the soul of Vrindavan. He loved to play in the forest. On one occasion he wanted to bathe with his friends in the Yamuna River, but she (river) was too far away. It appears that on this occasion the Yamuna had moved further away than Balarama liked. So he threatened her with his plough. She was afraid and immediately ran towards him, but not before he had scratched her banks and created small streams along them.

(9) Buddha Avatar (Mediatative Man)

*   All glories to you, O Lord of the universe, who took the form of Lord Buddha. Your heart is full of compassion for animals who were slaughtered in the ritual sacrifices of the Vedic-age.

In Buddha Avatar, Lord incarnates himself as Buddha, the ascetic prince who renounced the throne to lead the world on the part of peace. Most of the recorded teaching of Buddha, such as the Four Noble Truths and the Eight fold Path. He stopped the ritual slaughter of animals, and taught compassions to all living beings. As Buddha an enlightened man reiterated the importance of self-realization and self-effort in reading oneself.

(10) Kalki Avatar/The Destroyer (Supposed to be a mystical being)

*   All glories to you, O Lord of the universe, who will take the form of Kalki. Like a comet, you will appear riding a white horse and carrying a amazing sword. You will come to destroy all wicked people at the end of Kalki-Yuga.

* In the Vedic understanding of time, history passes in cycles of four yugas Satya, Treta, Dwapura and Kali. Satya Yuga is the age of goodness, but as such age passes goodness is replaced by passion and finally ignorance. By the end of Kali Yuga the present age almost all who remain of the human race will be sinful. The earth will be crowded with a corrupt population and terrorised by merciless rules. Plants and trees will be tiny. The bodies of all creatures will be reduced in size. Innocent people will be driven by famine and fear to hiden in the forests and mountains. At this time, nearly half- a-million years from now, Lord incarnates himself as Kalki. He will kill the cruel leaders and the thieves who support them. Then fragrant breezes will purify the world and the minds of the people, bringing Kali Yuga to an end. Those who remain will be left to populate the new golden age of Satya Yuga. Then the whole cycle will start again with to be characterized by truth, righteousness, and spiritual enlightenment. It will be a time of peace, prosperity, and harmony.

REFERENCES

1. ISKCON Educational Services The Heart of Hinduism.
2. Vedic feed The Complete List of 24 Avatars of Lord Krishna.
3. Krishna Today found in website

(E) ORIGIN OF LIFE AND ITS VALUE

*   (1) According to Vedic literature, Brahma, the creator of this universe, is considered the highest creator within the universe, but he is not God. That is stated that in Shrimad Bhagavatam : tene brahma hrda ya adi kavaya muhyanti yat surayah. God instructed him to create. Adi kavi : he is the original creator within the material world. Someone may question, "If he is not original creature, than how did he get his knowledge for creating ? "That is explained. Tene brahma hrda ya adikavaya Hrda means "heart." God instructed Brahma from within the heart.

(2) God is situated in everyone's heart. That form of God is called Paramatma.

> Ishwar Or Bhagavan means one endowed with unlimited opulence and refers to God who lives beyond this universe from spiritual realm as the Absolute Truth is one, without any duality, the origin of all origins (the personal feature of God).

i.   Brahman means the all-pervading universal soul, the concept of the transcendent and immanent ultimate reality (the impersonal feature of God).

ii. Atman means the individual soul or self; the thinking principle as manifested in consciousness and the size of soul is 1/10000 times the size of tip of hair (the eternal identity).

iii. Paramatma or Antaryami means the controller within and refers to God or Supersoul residing within the hearts of all beings (the localized feature of God).

iv. Jiva means the combination of body - mind , material and spirit - soul (the living entities or life being).

The Supreme Lord (Ishwar), the living entities (Jiva), the material nature (Prakriti), and the time (Kala) are all inter-related and are all eternal. The living entities as the superior energy and material nature as the inferior energy are both subordinate to the Supreme Personality of Godhead as the energetic. The material nature is created by Him, and the living entities are placed in this material nature, and thus all these activities and manifestations take place. Material nature itself is constituted by three qualities : the mode of goodness, the mode of passion, and the mode of ignorance. Above these modes there is the eternal time, and by a combination of these modes of nature and under the control and purview of the eternal time there are activities, which are called Karma. These activities are being carried out from time immemorial, and we are suffering or enjoying the fruits of our activities. Originally the living entities is a spiritual beings, but when he desires to enjoy this material world, he comes down.

(3) According to the Vedic conception, every planet contains living entities. That is natural to conclude, because within the material world everything is made of five gross elements : earth, water, fire, air, and sky. And the subtle elements are mind, intelligence, and ego. So in some planets, earth is prominent, in some planets, water is prominent, and in some planets, fire is prominent. Every planet in this material world is made of these five gross elements. Here we experience that some living entities are living in the water very peacefully. But if you are put into water, you will die. Similarly, if the fish are taken from the water, they will die on the land. Here we can see that some living entities can live comfortably on the land, some in the air. Similarly, why not some of them in fire. Because after all, fire is also one of the material elements. According to Vedic scripture there is life in the sun planet also. The living entities there have fiery bodies. That is all. That is the difference. Just as the fish here have bodies suitable for water, one may also have a fiery body. Logically we cannot deny that. We human beings have been given so many facilities by nature. There are so many living entities who must stand rooted to the ground for many years the trees, the plants. The aquatics are in the water for many, many years. The flies and insects remain in their condition for many, many years. And gradually, by the soul's evolution, we come to this form of human life.

(4) Chaitanya Mahaprabhu divided the living entities into two major categories : those that are moving and those that are not moving. Trees,

grass, plants, stones, etc., do not move because they do not have sufficiently developed consciousness. Their consciousness is there, but is covered. If a living beings does not understand his position, he is stone like, although dwelling in human body. The living entities birds, reptiles, animals, insects, human beings, demigods, etc. number over 8,400,000 species, and of these a very small number are human beings. There are 900, 000 species of acquatics, 2, 000, 000 species of trees and plants, 1, 100, 000 species of insects and reptiles, 1, 000, 000 species of birds, 3, 000, 000 species of animals bodies and 400, 000 human species. Lord Chaitanya further points out that out of 400,000 species of human beings, some are civilised ; and out of many civilised persons, there are only a few who are devoted to the scriptures.

(5) According to shastra (scripture), anyone who identifies himself with his body is a fool. That is the first instruction of the Bhagavat Gita. We all are spirit souls of supersoul from Godhead. As embodied soul continuously passes, in this body, from boyhood to youth to old age, the soul similarly passes, into another body at death. You have to change your body. Next you can get a cat body or a dog body, a tree body, or a demigod body, an American body, a serpent body any. There is no guarantee which body you will get. That will be awarded to you according to your karma (duties). This the highest message of religious and spiritual wisdom is that the human form of life is a matchless gift of God and it should be utilized to perfect human consciousness to realize the full meaning of life.

(6) Our real self, the soul is immortal. We may sleep for a little while in that change called death, but we can never be destroyed. We exist, and that existence is eternal. This body has come, and it will vanish ; but the soul essence to exist. Nothing can terminate that eternal consciousness. Even a particle of matter or a wave of energy is indestructible, as science has proved, the soul or spiritual essence of man is also indestructible. Matter undergoes change, the soul undergoes changing experiences. Radical changes are termed death, but death or a change in form does not change or destroy the spiritual essence.

(7) We will know that bodies of all living organisms primarily consist of four elements H (10%), O (61%), C (23%) and N (3%). Similarly, only a few types of molecules like water (67%), proteins (15%), lipids (13%), nucleic acids (<1%) and carbohydrates (1%) constitute 96% of all the molecules present in body of a living organism while minerals constitute about 4%. Many chemists and biologists feel that life is a product of the complex molecular reactions. In this paradigm it should be possible to create life within the laboratory. However, chemical evolutionists or neo-Darwinians face a very difficult task explaining the origin of life within their scientific framework. In other words, this material paradigm of life is not making much headway in an attempt to create life from a mixture of complex bio-molecules. It should be noted that if life is a product of complex molecular reactions, at this stage of scientific advancement a biochemist should be able to produce life in the laboratory. Since all the complex bio-molecules such as DNA, proteins, carbohydrates, lipids, etc., can be easily isolated, one does not need to start from small molecules. However, an honest person can see that a DNA molecule is not life and an enzyme or carbohydrate is not life.

From a holistic concept of life, we can see that material life, as we all know, has a physical body which is made up of (a) complex molecules (b) mind and intelligence and (c) a spiritual life particle called atma (soul). The body is thus animated by the presence of the atman. All the spiritual traditions proclaim that atman (life) is not made up of molecules. Rather it is beyond molecules. The body is meaningful so long as the atma is within the body. As stated earlier, molecules do not have meaning and value. Thus unless the spiritual dimension of life is known one cannot speak about the value of life, which includes peace. Our world-view and actions are very much dependent on our understanding of life. For a person following the materialistic paradigm on life, everything ends with death and thus his goal of life may be to pursue a life of materialistic enjoyment and accepts life to be of spiritual nature, strives for morality, peace and higher values in order to evolve into a higher level of consciousness. In this way, a paradigm shift from a materialistic to a spiritual paradigm will play a key role in pursuing and achieving a lasting world peace.

(8) Resolving Ethical Challenges and Achieving Word Peace

 Ethical are the fines qualities of human life from which human actions can be judged. Moral issues have always been closely connected with religious traditions. On the other hand, ethical values have never been seriously considered as part of science. This is primarily due to the emphasis on objectivity, reductionism and materialism in science. Biomedical issues like abortion and organ transplantation cannot be resolved unless we have a deeper understanding of life. According to the spiritual dimension of reality, material life begins at the moment of conception. Life is sacred and human life is very rarely obtained. In its pure form life is satcidananda. Sat means eternal, cit means full cognitive power and ananda means complete bliss. There can be no happiness without being peaceful. Thus spiritual life and peace go hand in hand. Furthermore, genuine faith in the existence of God will lead us to realize in the universal brotherhood, higher goals and deeper meaning and principles of life in order to achieving a lasting peace.

REFERENCES

1. ISKCON'S JOURNAL Bhagavat Message
2. Vedic Literature Texts

(F) ILLUSION AND MODES OF NATURE

* Maya means "that which is not." It refers to the Supreme Person's energy of illusion, which makes us think our temporary body, which is a product of the material world, is the same as our eternal, spiritual self, the atma within the body. When we are under Maya's influence, the attractive things in this world__wealth, fame, the opposite sex appear real and desirable to us. We think we should be able to enjoy and control them, as we like. But really, everything here is under the control of time, and none of these temporary things can bring us lasting happiness. Everything about Krishna, the Supreme Person, is completely spiritual. He always has been and always will be the supreme controller and enjoyer. But when we want to enjoy or control separately from Him __ as if we were God ourselves__everything then appears to us as material, non-spiritual , separate from God, and exploitable. What we see then is maya, illusion, because in reality nothing is separate from the Absolute Truth, the Supreme Person, Krishna.

Maya The Nature of Illusion

* Maya has three attributes : Sattva, Rajas, and Tamas (goodness, passion and ignorance). These attributes are just like chains used to tie up the ungrateful souls. Maya then applies a double case on spiritual form of the soul. The double case described by the word linga and sthula. The mayik existence has twenty-four substances :

1. Five Gross (visible) Elements are (a) Earth Like the earth, Our body also has soil particles as a component. (b) Water Like the earth, Our body also has water as a component. (c) Fire Like the earth, Our body also has heat (fire) as a component. (d) Air Like the earth, Our body also has air as a component and (e) Ether Like the earth, Our body also has empty space as component.

2. Five Knowledge Acquiring Senses (Gnanendriyas) are (a) Eyes see the objects (b) Nose smells the fragrance (c) Ear hear the sound (d) Mouth - feels the taste and speaks the knowledge and (e) Skin feels

the touch (perception). These five elements acquire knowledge from outside.

3. Five Subtle Elements (the objects known by the five Gnanendriyas) are (a) Sight (b) Smell (c) Sound (d) Taste and (e) Touch (perception).

4. Five Working Senses (a) Hands (b) Legs (c) Mouth (d) Rectum and (e) Genitals. These above twenty elements form the sthul-deha or outer case.

5. Four Subtle (invisible) Elements are (a) Mind (the mana) (b) Intelligence (the budhi) (c) False - ego (1. the chitta and 2. the ahankar, i.e. the attention and the perverted ego). These four compose the linga-deha or inner case.

After encasing the spiritual form of the soul, Maya employs the fallen souls to work. Mayik work is composed of karma, akarma, and vikarma. Karma is conventionally good action done to obtain virtue, such as the performance of duties enjoyed by the devotees who follow scriptures. Akarma is the omission to do duty. Vikarma is sin and crime.

Karma procures heavenly elevations up to the Brahmaloka planet. Akarma gives an unpleasant state on earth. Vikarma hurls down souls to hell. The fallen souls travels from body to body with their lingadeha doing karma or vikarma, rising up to the heavens, and again coming down at the exhaustion of their virtues, going down to hell, and after suffering punishment, again rising up to the platform of work. Thus the state of the fallen souls is deplorable in the extreme. They enjoy or suffer massacre and murder, and go on in this state, sometimes smiling as the princess and sometimes suffering in ruins. The world is, therefore, a prison or a house of correction, and not a place for enjoyment as some people assert.

Modes of Material Nature

(1) Everyone should know how God, or Lord Krishna, is great, and everyone should know the factual position of the living entities. Everyone should know that a living entity is eternally a servant and

unless one serves Krishna one has to serve illusion in different varieties of the three modes of material nature and thus wander perpetually within the cycle of birth and death; even so-called liberated Mayavadi speculator has undergo this process. This knowledge constitutes a great science, and each and every living being has to hear it for his own interest.

(2) In the Gita it is clearly mentioned that material energy works fully under the direction of the Supreme Lord. It has no independent authority. It works as the shadow moves, in accordance with the movements of the object. But still material energy is very powerful, and the atheist, due to his godless temperament, cannot know how it works ; nor can he know the plan of the Supreme Lord. Under illusion and the modes of passion and ignorance, all his plans are baffled, as in the case of Hiranyakshipu and Ravana, whose plans were smashed to although they were both materially learned as scientists, philosophers, administrators and educators.

(3) When there is an increase in the mode of ignorance darkness, inertia, madness, and illusion are manifested When there is no illumination, knowledge is absent. One in the mode of ignorance does not work by a regulative principle ; he wants to act whimsically for no purpose. Even though he has capacity to work, he makes no endeavor. This is called illusion. Although consciousness is going on, life is inactive. These are the symptoms of one in the mode of ignorance.

(4) The result of pious activities in the mode of goodness is pure. Therefore the sages, who are free from all illusion are situated in happiness. But activities in the mode of passion are simply miserable. Any activity for material happiness is bound to be defeated. If, for example, one wants to have a skyscraper, so much human misery has to be undergone before a big skyscraper can be built. The financier has to take much trouble to earn a mass of wealth and those who are slaving to construct the building have to render physical toil. The miseries are there. Thus Bhagavat-Gita says that in any activity performed under the spell of the mode of

passion, there is definitely great misery. There may be a little so-called mental happiness ' I have this house or this money' but this is not actual happiness.

(5) Pure goodness is transcendental ; in purified goodness one can understand the real nature of the Supreme Personality of Godhead. As long as one's faith is not completely in purified goodness, the faith is subject to contamination by any of the modes of material nature. The contaminated modes of material nature expand to the heart. Therefore accordingly to the position of the heart in contact with a particular mode of material nature, one's faith is established. It should be understood that if one's heart is in the mode of goodness his faith is also in the mode of goodness. If his heart is in the mode of passion, his faith is also in the mode of passion. And if his heart is in the mode of darkness, illusion, his faith is also thus contaminated. Thus we find different types of faith in the world, and there are different types of religions due to different types of faiths. The real principles of religious faith is situated in the mode ofpure goodness, but because the heart is tainted we find different types of religious principles. Thus according to different types of faith, there are different kinds of worship.

(6) One has to give account of one's actions to the state or to the agents of the Supreme Lord called the Yamadutas. Irresponsible work is destructive because it destroys the regulation principles of scriptural injunction. It is often based on violence and is distressing to other living entities. Such irresponsible work is carried out in the light of one's personal experience. This is called illusion. And all such illusory work is a product of the mode of ignorance.

(7) One who takes pleasure in laziness and in sleep is certainly in the mode of darkness, ignorance and one who has no idea how to act and how not to act is also in the mode of ignorance. For the person in the mode of ignorance, everything is illusion. There is no happiness either in the beginning or at the end. For the person in the mode of passion there might be some kind of ephemeral happiness in the beginning and at the end distress, but for the

person in the mode of ignorance there is only distress both in the beginning and at the end.

(8) In the material sky everything is relative truth. That is to say, one truth depends on something else. This cosmic creation results from interaction of the three modes of nature, and the temporary manifestations are so created as to present an illusion of reality to the bewildered mind of the conditioned soul, who appears in so many species of life, including the higher demigods, like Brahma, Indra, Candra, and so on. In actuality, there is no reality in the manifested world. There appears to be reality, however, because of the true reality which exists in the spiritual world, where the Personality of Godhead eternally exists with His transcendental paraphernalia.

(9) The material creation is meant for rebellious souls who are not prepared to accept subordination under the Supreme Lord. This spirit of false lordship is called false ego. It is manisfested in the three modes of material nature, and it exists in mental speculation only. Those who are in the mode of goodness think that each and every person of God, and thus they laugh at the pure devotees, who try to engage in the transcendental loving service of the Lord. Those who are puffed up by the mode of passion try to lord it over material nature in various ways. Some of them engage in altruistic activities as if they were against appointed to do good to others by their mental speculative plans. Such men accept the standard ways of mundane altruism, but their plans are made on the basis of false ego. This false ego extends to the limit of becoming one with the Lord. The last class of egoistic conditioned souls those in the mode of ignorance are misguided by identification of the gross body with the self. Thus, all their activities are centered around the body only. All these persons are given the chance to play with false egoistic ideas, but at the same time the Lord is kind enough to give them a chance to take help from scriptures like Bhagavat-Gita and Shrimad-Bhagavatam so that they may understand the science of God and thus make their lives successful. The entire material creation, therefore, is meant for the false egoistic living entities

hovering on the mental plane under different illusion in the modes of material nature.

(10) It is a most ludicrous argument to say that the Supreme Lord is overpowered by His own material energy. The Lord is master of the material energy, but the living entities are in the conditioned state, controlled by the material energy. That is the version of Bhagavat-Gita. The froggish philosophers who put forward the argument that the Supreme Lord overpowered by the material mode of goodness are themselves illusioned by the same material energy, although they think of themselves as liberated souls. They support their arguments by a false and laborious jugglery of words, which is a gift of the same illusory energy of the Lord. But the poor froggish philosophers, due to a false sense of knowledge, cannot understand the situation.

(11) The energy emanated from the Supreme Personality of Godhead manifest in two ways as an emanation from the Supreme Lord and as a covering of the Lord's face. In Bhagavat-Gita it is said that because the whole world is illusioned by the three modes of material nature, the common conditioned soul, being covered by such energy, cannot see the Supreme Personality of Godhead. The example of a cloud is very nicely given. All of a sudden there may appear a big cloud in the sky. This cloud is perceived in two ways. To the sun the cloud is a creation of its energy, but to the ordinary common man in the conditioned state, it is a covering to the eyes ; because of the cloud, the sun cannot be seen. It is not that the sun is actually covered by the cloud ; only the vision of the ordinary being is covered. Similarly, although maya cannot cover the Supreme Lord, who is beyond maya, the material energy covers the ordinary living entities. Those conditioned souls who are covered are individual living entities and He from whose energy maya is created the Supreme Personality of Godhead.

(12) In this material world there is a great illusion which covers real intelligence. A man in the mode of passion wants to work very

hard to derive some benefit, but he does not know that time will never allow him to enjoy anything permanently.

(13) When one becomes angry, he forgets himself and his situation, but if one is able to consider his situation by knowledge, one transcends the influence of the modes of material nature. One is always a servant of lusty desires, anger, greed, illusion, envy and so forth, but if one obtains sufficient strength in spiritual advancement, one can control them. One who obtain such control will always be transcendentally situated, untouched by the modes of material nature. This is only possible when one fully engages in the service of the Lord.

(14) In the world of duality that is to say, in the material world so called goodness and badness are both the same Therefore, in this world, to distinguish between good and bad, happiness and distress, is meaningless because they are both mental concoctions (manodharma). Because everything here is miserable and troublesome, to create an artificial situation and pretend it to be full of happiness is simply illusion. The liberated person, being above the influence of the three modes of material nature, is unaffected by such dualities in all circumstances. He remains devotional service by tolerating so-called happiness and distress.

REFERENCED

Vaniquotes the compiled essence of Vedic Knowledge.

(G) ETHICS AND COSMIC ORDER (VEDIC SCIENCE)

* Sampradayas means those who carefully follow the Vedic principles. The Vedic literature includes the four Vedas, the Upanishads, the Puranas, the Ramayana, the Vedanta-sutra, then Shrimad-Bhagavatam is the explanation of the Vedanta-sutra. Therefore at the end of each chapter of the Shrimad-Bhagavatam Vyasadeva states, brahma-sutrasya bhasha : "The Shrimad-Bhagavatam is commentary on the Brahma-sutra." Brahma-sutra or Vedanta-sutra, gives the gist of the Vedic literature in the codes. And the Shrimad-Bhagavatam explains these codes. The Vedanta-sutra begin, athato brahma jijnasa. "Now is the time inquire into the Absolute Truth." And the Shrimad-Bhagavatam states, jivasya tattva jijnasa : "The only business for living beings is to inquire about the Absolute Truth." That is the only business. People are trouble because they have given up their real business. Human life is meant for this business brahma jijnass, to inquire about the Absolute Truth. The human form of life is considered to be superior to the other forms of life by all thinkers. The Vedic culture this view and its tells us that the human form of life is the means to achieve the supreme benefit of one's existence. For those who are interested in progress there are some guidelines in the form of conduct rules. The most important question which arises at this point is the authority of the power who lays down these conduct rules. Of course, we are all acquainted with different sects governed by different codes of conduct, laid down by their founders or governors, Vedic Culture, however, accepts the authority of the Supreme personality of Godhead and no other individual opinion. Vedic truths should, then, be accepted as the only truths in higher matters. Reason, while sincerely helping inspired truth, may be accepted as auxiliary evidence. The Vedas teach us, according to Chaitanya Mahaprabhu, nine principal doctrines, which are :

(1) Hari, the Almighty, is one without a second.

(2) He is always vested with infinite power.

(3) He is the ocean of rasa (the transcendental bliss which forms the essence of any relationship)

(4) The soul is His vibhinnamsha or separated part.

(5) Certain souls are engrossed by prakriti His illusory energy.

(6) Certain souls are released from the grasp of prakriti.

(7) All spiritual and material phenomena are bhedabheda prakash of Hari, the Almighty (simultaneously one and different with the Lord)

(8) Bhakti, devotional service, is the only the final object of spiritual existence.

(9) Prema, pure love in Krishna, is alone the final object of spiritual existence.

Vedic Cosmology of Understanding the Four Yugas

* According to Vedic philosophy, the world is made up of four main "Yugas" ages, epochs, or cycles of time each made up of tens of thousands of human years. Yugas in the Vedic texts that are millions of years old but written down over 5000 years ago is an epoch or era within a four age cycle. A complete Yuga starts with the Satya Yuga via Treta Yuga and Dvapara Yuga into a Kali Yuga. Our present time is a Kali, which started at 3120 B.C.E. with the end of the Mahabharata war. Kali-Yuga will continue on for 432,000 years of which we have passed through the first 5000 years. According to the laws of Vedic cosmology, the Universe is created wholly, only to be destroyed entirely, once in every 4•1 to 8•2 billion years. This is believed to constitude one full day and night for Lord Brahma, the creator of the universe. One Brahma's lifetime is considered to be a around 311 trillion and 40 billion human years. These yugas are believed to repeat themselves in cyclical patterns, much like the waxing and waning of the moon like the four seasons, like the rising and ebbing of tides.

The Shrimad-bhagavatam indicates that the duration of the Satya Yuga is equivalent to about 4,800 years of the Demigods, the duration of the

Treta Yuga is about 3,600 years, the duration of the Dvapara Yuga is 2,400 years ; and that of the Kali Yuga is about 1,200 years of the demigods. Hence, one could probably infer from these statistics that one year of a demigod would be the equivalent of about 360 human years.

This would also be lead us to believe the Satya Yuga lasted for 4,800 × 360, that is, about 1,728,000 years. The Treta Yuga, on the other hand, went on for 3,600 × 360 years, which works out 1,296,000 years. Similarly, the Dvapara Yuga continued for 2,400 × 360, that is 864,000 years The Kali Yuga is supposed to be the shortest of them all, lasting for only 1,200 × 360 years, which totals to 432,000 years. From the aforementioned statistic, it can be understood that the four Yugas follow a timeline ratio of 4 : 3 : 2 : 1.

According to the Laws of Manu, the length of each Yuga is 4800 years + 3600 years + 2400 years + 1200 years, which equals 12,000 years. This figure denotes only a half cycle and hence, the entire cycle takes 24,000 years to complete. This is also one precession of the equinox.

The current Universe is, according to Vedic scripture, in the 51st year of Brahma's life, which suggests that it was created about 155•5 trillion years ago. This figure does not match the modern day small estimated age of the universe of 13•79 billion years.

Characteristics of above Four Yugas

(1) Satya / Krita Yuga (the age of divine souls) : The first and best Yuga. It is the age of truth and perfection. Caste system is very flexible. Brahmanas are capable of achieving miracles by mere fiat of will Kshatriyas are endowed with superhuman physical powers. Human are gigantic, powerful built, handsome, honest, youthful, vigorous, erudite and virtuous. The Vedas are one. There is no agriculture nor mining as the earth yields those riches on its own. Weather is pleasant and everyone is happy. There is no religious sect. In the earlier part of the Yuga, all humans were Brahmanas and live as sibling. There was no disease, decrepitude or fear of

anything. There was no music, song, dance, buying or selling. There was no disparity among cultures. No animals were slain in sacrifices. There was no city, town, or nation. There was no war, famine, conflict among the human race. It was a time of complete peace on earth. In the later part of the Yuga, civilization is established and the Brahmanas, Kshatriyas, Vaishyas and Sudras perform their duties well. Human lifespan is 100,000 years and humans tend to have hundreds or thousands of sons or daughters. People must perform penances for thousands of years to acquire Samadhi and die. It is believed that the Dharma Bull, which embodies the quality of morality, stood on all four legs of austerity, purity, mercy, and truth, during this period. It was sometimes referred to as the "Golden Age."

(2) Treta Yuga (the age of intelligent beings) : Treta means second. In this age, virtue diminishes slightly. At the beginning of the age, many emperors rise to dominance and conquer the world. War become frequent and weather begins to change to extremities. Oceans and deserts are formed. Majority Brahmanas become slightly less powerful. People are divided into various cultures and people of mixed classes are born. People become slightly diminished compared to their predecessors. Agriculture, labour and mining become existent. Significant people born in this age include Rama, Lakshman, Hanuman, Dasharatha, etc. Average age of human is around 1000 -10,000. Although there was some division among society, it was nevertheless a time of overarching peace and prosperity. It is believed that the Dharma Bull, which embodies the quality of morality, stood on three legs, during this period. It is sometimes referred to as the "Silver Age."

(3) Dvapara Yuga (the age of mental beings) : Dvapara Yuga is the third age. In this age, people become tainted with Tamasic (ignorance) qualities and are not strong as their ancestors. Disease become rampant. Humans are discontent and fight each other. Vedas are divided into four parts. People still possess characteristics of youth in old age. Significant people born in this age are Krishna, Balarama, the Pandavas, the Kauravas, Shantanu, Bhishma, Drona,

Karna, Draupadi, Kunti, Abhimanu, etc. Average age is around a few centuries or up to 1,000 years. It is believed that the Dharma Bull, which embodies the quality of morality, stood on two legs, during this period. It is sometimes referred to as the "Bronze Age."

(4) Kali Yuga (the age of physical beings) : It is the age of darkness and ignorance. People become sinners and lack virtue. They become slaves to their passions and are barely as powerful as their earliest ancestors in the Satya Yuga. Knowledge is lost and scriptures are diminished. Humans eat forbidden and dirty food and engage in unrestrained sinful sexual practices. The environment is polluted, water and food become scarce. Wealth is heavily diminished. Brahmanas become ignorant, Kshatriyas become weak, Vaishya employ questionable business tactics and Sudras treacherously acquire power. Families become non-existent. Average age of people is barely 100 years though by the end of the Yuga, it will be up to 20 years only. At present, in the immortal age of Kali, (the Goddess of time , doomsday and death), the Dharma Bull is believed to be standing only on one leg. It is sometimes referred to as the "Iron Age."

Metaphorically, the four Yuga ages may symbolize the four phases of involution during which the human gradually lost the awareness of his or her inner selves and subtle bodies. In Vedic concept, human beings have five kinds of bodies, known as 1. the gross body 2. the breath body 3. the psychic body 4. the intelligence body and 5. The bliss body.

Time and New Year

* Let's begin with the word "Year." A year is a unit for measuring time. And what is time? Though the reality of time, especially in the form of its effect on us, is undeniable, time is one among the many fundamental truths of life that defy scientific definition. Be that as it may, we measure time by the movement of the cosmic bodies. As per current scientific understanding one year is the time in which the earth completes one revolution around the sun. For an object

orbiting continuously in a circular path, no point on the orbit can be considered special. So scientifically there's nothing "new" about the new year, the earth is going to continue in its same old path! In our society today, we are striving not to repeat the mistakes of the past. We wish to grow beyond time. We have been brought by the wave of time. The cyclical theory of Social Change would take the analogy of the physical world. The sun rises after every twenty four hours, makes, thereby, a cycle of day and night.

The Vedic scriptures explain that all living beings eat, mate, sleep and defend. In fact, the subhuman beings do nothing but these four activities. And modern man is also doing just these four activities, although in a sophisticated way. Even the entire gamut of scientific advancement is impelled by these four fundamental drives. Unbelievable ? Let's see how. The first thing that man did after unravelling the mysteries of the atom to use the atomic bomb defence in the most horrendous form seen in the contemporary times. The result of the advent of information age is interest, which is mostly an international network of gossip about pornography that's mating in its grossest form. The leaps ingenetic engineering have mostly been actuated by desire for better meat and other foodstuffs is anything higher than eating? Dunlop beds, nowadays water beds, charger beds, robot woman, and what not they are all obviously for sleeping. So a little thought will reveal how all the "advanced" activities done by the modern man eventually boil down to eating, sleeping, mating and defending. And there's nothing new in them, no matter how we do them externally. The Bhagavatam describes this in graphic terms : punah punas carvita carvananam "Chewing the chewed."

Therefore the Vedic scriptures encourage us to sublimate our attraction for the new by directing it to the realm of spirit. "athato brahma jijnasa" the first aphorism of the Vedanta-sutra is a clarion call to all its readers : "Therefore inquire about the higher dimensions of life." It is quite surprising to see a book starting with the word 'therefore.' The implication is, "Now, O spirit soul, who has acquired a human body, cease from the animal business of eating, sleeping, mating and defending. Now you are endowed with a higher intelligence in the human form. Therefore inquire about the higher truths of life." And this higher enquiry is not fruitless armchair speculation. The answers to it constitute a practical way of life which bestows upon the seeker unlimited happiness from the spiritual stratum. And this is in fact the Vedic mission : sarve janah sukhino bhavanta Let everyone be happy not superficially and temporarily by success in the rat race for sense gratification, but deeply and eternally by absorption in loving service to God.

Spiritual life culminates in the development of love of God, the Universal Father, precipitates love for all living beings as one's own brothers. This selfless love completely satisfies the self and also makes the lovers of God the topmost welfare worker for all living beings. Love of God is our original and real nature, but due to prolonged and excessive conduct with matter, it has become completely obscured and is now misdirected towards various material objects. All genuine spiritual practices are meant to revive this love of God, which is presently dormant is our hearts. And God being infinite is eternally new and so living Him is an eternally new and happy experience. Thus revival of our love of God is the ultimate fruition of the wish "Happy New Year !"

REFERENCE

1. The Vedic Scripture Texts
2. The Message of Bhagavata (Magazine)

(H) THE VEDIC SYSTEM OF CIVILIZATION

Varnashrama dharma

The Dharma conveyed in the Vedas is based on two points varna and ashram together called varnashrama dharma. Thus the term 'Varnashrama dharma' is made up of three words (1) varna (2) ashrama and (3) dharma. Theoretically, the Varna system refers to the segmental division of the Vedic Culture into four social groups according to one's natural talents and propensities. The Ashram system refers to the segmental division of ideal life span of an individual into four stages. Dharma refers to the duty of an individual. Ideal Varnashrama dharma system of life suggests certain duties of an individual as a member of society relating to their stage of life. It does not depend on social status, temperament of specific power and capacities. Varnashrama dharma is the Vedic Culture of the Goals of life, Social divisions and Stages of life and one is encouraged to strive for a balance and harmony of all the four goals and not to neglect one in favour of the others.

Thus Varnashrama dharma is the combination of the Four-Varnas, Four Ashrams and Four Dharmas:

The Four Varnas

(1) Brahmana (The Intelligentsia), (2) Kshatriya (The Administrators), (3) Vaishya (The Entrepreneur), and (4) Sudra (The Proletariate). As useful analogy the social body and its components are likened to the human form. Society is compared to a body with the brahmanas as the head (brain), kshatriyas as the arms, vaishya, as the belly (or thighs) and the sudras as the legs. Social functions are determined according to this analogy. For example, the brahmanas are the eyes and mouth of the society. They provide a spiritual vision for society and teach people accordingly. Just as the arms are raised to defend the body, the kshatriya's main duty is to protect society. The vaishya's main duty is to material nourishment (productive and trading) and the sudra supports all the other sections of society. These four classes of human are prevalent

everywhere under different names. Originally, these four classes were determined by the capacity and profession of the individual not by birth. The duties of these classes are determined according to inborn quality and nature. Because it is created by the original creator, so it is prevalent everywhere.

Four Ashrams

(1) Brahmacarin (Student), (2) Grihasta (Householder), (3) Vanprastha (Retiree), and (4) Sanyasi (Renunciate). During the stage of studentship one learns the principles of Dharma ----- spiritual wisdom, religious duties as well as secular knowledge. During the stage of the householder this sacred and secular knowledge is put into practice. One then indulges in sensual pleasures and procreation (kama) and accumulates wealth (artha) in accordance with religious principles (dharma) to support one's family and distributes the surplus in philanthropic acts. In the stage of the retirement a process of preparing for eventual renunciation is began and one gradually abandons one's profession and sense-enjoyment, and concentrates on dharma with a view to achieve Liberation (Moksha) from the cycle of birth and death. When one finally renounces (sanyas) then one's complete focus is on obtaining Liberation (Moksha) to the exclusion of all else as the stage of Sanyasi. The Brahmins are expected to pass through all these four stages. Kshatriyas pass through all these first three, Vaishya have the first two and the Sudras have the one stage that of householder. These are the general recommendations but not practice there are many exceptions.

The Four Dharmas

(1) Righteousness, Duties and Ethics (Dharma)
(2) Desire of work for wealth and prosperity (Artha)
(3) Pursuit of desires that make one happy, love, sensual desires and passions (Kama) and
(4) Enlightenment or Salvation (Moksha).

Among all of these four Dharmas, righteousness (dharma) is most essential, since either Artha or Kama pursued outside the restraints of Dharma (righteousness) will only lead to ruin.

Lastly, Varnashrama dharma is a great one. It works as a principle of spiritual unity amongst the four classes not to forget that it is also an excellent mechanism of social adjustment. No society can flourish unless its members realise the duties and perform the sincerely since according to the Vedic literature, Varnashrama dharma is not a man-made system.

VEDIC RULES OF LIFE : A WAY TO LEAD PEACEFUL LIFE.

Vedic traditions should be practiced towards those who genuinely respect Vedic values. Vedic humanistic values are shown towards human not inhuman people who hate peace, love and advocate terrorism to spread their cultism. Vedic principles are ways to lead life in peaceful manner with prosperity and happiness. It does not say that some section of peoples alone should follow these rules, these are for humans. In the seventh canto of Shrimad bhagwatam king Yudhishthir asks sage Narada to describe the conduct rules conducive to the welfare and benefit of human beings. Sage Narada describes what he learnt from sage Narayana, the Supreme Personality of Godhead. There are thirty conduct rules which apply to all human beings irrespective of caste, creed, age, sex and situation in life. They are given below in serial order with some explanation :

(1) Satyam (Truthfulness)

Adhere to truthfulness, refraining from lying and betraying promises. Speak only that which is true, kind, helpful and necessary. Knowing that deception creates distance, don't keep secrets from family or loved ones. Be fair, accurate and frank in discussions, a stranger to deceit. Admit your failings. Do not engage in slander, gossip or backbiting. Do not bear false witness against another.

(2) Daya (Compassion or Kindness)

Practice compassion, conquering callous, cruel and insensitive feelings toward all beings. See God everywhere. Be kind to people, animals, plants and the Earth itself. Forgive those who apologize and show true remorse. Foster sympathy for other's needs and suffering. Honour and assist those who are weak, impoverished, aged or in pain. Oppose family abuse and other cruelties.

(3) Tapah (Austerity)

Practice austerity, serious disciplines, penance and sacrifice Be arden in worship, meditation and pilgrimage. Atone for misdeeds through penance, such as 108 prostrations or fasting. Perform self-denial, giving up cherished possessions, money or time. Fulfill severe austerities at special times, under a satguru's (bonafide master) guidance, to ignite the inner fires of self-transformation.

(4) Saucam (Purity)

Uphold the ethic of purity, avoiding impurity in mind, body and speech. Maintain a clean, healthy body, keep a pure, uncluttered home and workplace. Act virtuosly. Keep good company, never mixing with adulterers, thieves or other impure people. Keep away from pornography and violence. Never use harsh, angered or indirect language. Worship devoutly. Mediate daily.

(5) Titiksha (Tolerance)

One should bear with pleasant and unpleasant changes, which happen as a course of life.

(6) Iksha

Distinguishing what is right and what is wrong.

(7) Samah

Control over mental impulses.

(8) Damah

Control over bodily impulses.

(9) Ahimsa : (Non-violence)

Non-violence by not causing mental or physical suffering to others. Practice non-injury, not harming others by thought, word or deed, even in our dreams. Live a kindly life, revering all beings as expressions of the

One Divine energy. Let go of fear and insecurity, the sources of abuse. Knowing that harm caused to others unfailingly returns to oneself, live peacefully with God's creation. Never be a source of dread, pain or injury. Follow a vegetarian diet.

(10) Brahmacaryam (Celibacy)

Practice divine conduct, controlling lust by remaining celibate when single and faithful in marriage. Before marriage, use vital energies in study and after marriage in creating family success. Don't waste the sacred force by promiscuity in thought, word or deed. Be restrained with opposite sex. Seek holy company. Dress and speak modestly. Shun pornography, sexual humor and violence.

(11) Tyagah

One should Whole-heartedly give up claims over one's possessions and achievements.

(12) Svadhayaya (Study of Scriptures)

Eagerly hear the scriptures, study the teachings and listen to the wise of your lineage. Choose a guru (spiritual master), follow his path and don't waste time exploring other ways. Read, study and above all, listen to reading and dissertations by which wisdom flows from knower to seeker. Avoid secondary text that preach violence. Revere and study the revealed scriptures, the Vedas and Agamas.

(13) Arjavam (Straight-forwardness)

Maintain honesty, renouncing deception and wrongdoing. Act honourably even in hard times. Obey the laws of your nation and local. Pay your taxes. Be straightforward in business. Do an honest day's work. Do not bribe or accept bribes. Do not cheat, deceive or circumvent to achieve an end. Be frank with yourself. Face and accept your faults without blaming them on others.

(14) Santosh (Contentment)

Nature contentment, seeking joy and serenity in life. Be happy, smile and uplift others. Live in constant gratitude for your health, your friends and your belongings. Don't complain about what you don't possess. Identify with the eternal. You, rather than mind the mountaintop view that life is an opportunity for spiritual progress. Live in the eternal now.

(15) Samadrik Seva

One should render service to noble and saintly persons who treat all in the same way. Where one is rendering service one should not expect preferential treatment or favouritism.

(16) Gramychoparatih Sanah

Gradually withdrawing from all mundane activities.

(17) Nrnam (Nrinam) Viparyayeheksha

One should see how the worldly pursuits of people in general do not yield the desired results. What is more the result will be contrary to the expectations.

(18) Maunam

Refraining from gossip. We usually associate this with remaining silent. A muni (sage) is one who has complete mastering over his speech.

(19) Atmavirmarsanam

Apparently this means introspection. However, here it implies enquiry about one's real identity which leads to the understanding of distinction between body and soul.

(20) Annadhyadeh Samvibhago Bhute Bhyarca Yatharatah

The means of livelihood life etc. should be divided among all beings according to merit. One should not be satisfied by feeding one self.

(21) Tesvatme Devata Buddhish Sutaram NRSU.

One should regard all beings as one's own self and see the divinity inherent in all. This outlook has to be cultivated specially in the case of fellow human beings.

(22), (23), and (24) Asy Mahatam Gateh Sravanam Kirtanam Smaranam

The Supreme Personality of Godhead is the refuge of all great souls. Therefore one should hear about the Lord's glories, chant the names of the Lord and endeavour (try) to constantly dwell on the name, form, glory, etc of the Lord.

(25) Seva

Devotional Service by way of offering services.

(26) Ijya

Formal worship.

(27) Avanatiha

Bowing down showing one's humility and regard to the Lord.

(28) Dasyam

Service like a bonded labourer. This is rather a very advanced form of service. Hanuman is serving Lord Rama's our guide.

(29) Sakhyam

Apparently it means friendship. We all know that friendship is a kind of relationship between near equals. Arjuna realises this and prays for forgiveness. Sakhyam means accepting the Lord as our eternal companion (The supersoul of the individual soul).

(30) Atma samarpanam

Offering the self-lock stock and barrel to the supreme personality of Godhead. These thirty qualities have to be cultivated by all human beings to gain perfection of life.

Some Vedic Restraints (Yama)

(1) Non-stealing (Asteya)

Uphold the virtue of non-stealing, neither thieving, coveting nor failing to repay debt. Control your desires and live within your means. Do not use borrowed resources for unintended purposes or keep them past due. Do not gamble or defraud others. Do not renege on promises. Do not use other's name, words, resources or rights without permission and acknowledgement.

(2) Patience ((Kshama)

Exercise patience, restraining intolerance with people and impatience with circumstances. Be agreeble. Let others behave according to their nature, without adjusting to you. Don't argue, dominate conversations or interrupt others. Don't be in a hurry. Be patient with children and the elderly. Minimize stress by keeping worries at bay. Remain poised in good times and bad.

(3) Steadfastness (Dhriti)

Foster steadfastness, overcoming non-perseverance, fear, indecision and changeableness. Achieve your goals with a prayer, purpose, plan, persistence and push. Be firm in your decisions. Avoid sloth and procrastination. Develop will-power, courage and industriousnes. Overcome obstacles. Never carp or complain. Do not let opposition or fear of failure result in changing strategies.

(4) Moderate Appetite (Mitahara)

Be moderate in appetite, do not eat too much and never consume meat, fish, shell-fish, fowl or eggs. Enjoy fresh, whole-some vegetarian foods that vitalize the body. Avoid junk food. Drink juices in moderation. Eat at regular times. Only when hungry, at a moderate pace, never between meals, in a disturbed atmosphere or when upset. Follow a simple diet, avoiding rich or fancy fare.

OTHER SOME VEDIC OBSERVANCES (NIYAM)

(1) Remorse (Hri)

All yourself the expression of remorse, being modest and showing shame for misdeeds. Recognize your errors, confess and make amends. Sincerely apologize to those hurt by your words or deeds. Resolve all contention before sleep. Seek out and correct your faults and bad habits. Welcome correction as a means to bettering yourself. Do not boast. Shun pride and pretension.

(2) Giving (Dana)

Be generous to a fault, giving liberally without thought of reward. Tithe, offering one-tenth of your gross income, as God's money, to temples, ashrams and spiritual organizations. Approach the temple with offerings. Visit guru with gifts in hand. Donate religious literature. Feed and give to those in need. Bestow your time and talents without seeking praise Treat guest as God.

(3) Faith (Astikya)

Cultivate an unshakable faith. Believe firmly in God, Gods, guru and your path to enlightenment. Trust in the words of the masters, the scriptures and traditions. Practice devotion and sadhana to inspire experiences that build advanced faith. Be loyal to your lineage, one try to break your faith by argument and accusation. Avoid doubt and despair.

(4) Worship (Ishvarpuja)

Cultivate devotion through daily worship and meditation. Set aside one room of your home as God's shrine. Offer fruits, flowers or foods daily. Learn a simple puja and chants. Meditate after each puja visit your shrine before and after leaving the house. Worship in heartfelt devotion, clearing the inner channels to God, God's and guru so their flows toward you and loved ones.

(5) Cognition (Mati)

Develop a spiritual will and intellect with your satguru's guidance. Strive for knowledge of God, to awaken the light within. Discover the hidden lesson in each experience to develop a profound understanding of life and yourself. Through meditation, cultivate intuition by listening to the still, small voice within, by understanding the subtle sciences, inner worlds and mystical text.

(6) Sacred Vows (Vrata)

Embrace religious vows, rules and observances and never waver in fulfilling them. Honour vows as spiritual contracts with your soul, your community, with God, Gods and guru. Take vows to harness the instinctive nature. Fast periodically. Pilgrimage yearly. Uphold your vows strictly, be they marriage, monasticism, tithing, loyalty to a lineage, vegetarianism or non-smoking.

(7) Recitation (Japa)

Chant your holy mantra daily, reciting the sacred sound, word or phrase given by your guru. Bathe first, quiet the mind and concentrate fully to let japa harmonize, purify and uplift you. Heed your instructions and chant the prescribed repetitions without fail. Live free of anger so that japa strengthens your higher nature. Let japa quell emotions and quiet the river of thought.

REFERENCE

1. Vedic Literature Texts
2. Varnashrama dharma -Ved-Wikidot

(I) DEVOTEE AND DEVOTIONAL SERVICE

(1) Devotional Service As Bhagavat-Culture

* The meaning of Bhagavata or Devotee the worshipper or follower of Bhagavan, Lord Shri Krishna, the form of service is called Bhakti or Devotion. Thus the Bhagavat-Culture is about the deeper meaning of life and universe as the concept is woven around the transcendental knowledge of Shrimad-Bhagvat-Gita and Shrimad-Bhagvatam (Bhagavat- Purana), the ripened fruit of the tree of Vedic literatures. The Sanskrit word "Bhagavata" means pertaining to Bhagavan, the Supreme Being who possesses all opulence in full is known as 'Bhagavan' and Bhagavat-Culture is the art of dovetailing all human endeavours in the service of the Lord. Bhagavat-Culture further teaches that whatever talent, ability or skill we may possess can be used in the glorification of the Supreme Lord since the main focus depends upon moral and spiritual values through applied spiritual science and technology as realised by the Bhagavata sages. The vision of a devotee for a better world, is a world in which everyone is educated to realise that this human form of life is the most important gift of the Supreme Lord.

* Devotional Service means activities performed for the transcendental pleasure of Supreme Lord Shri Krishna, with devotion, and ultimately not mixed with any desire for personal pleasure. Devotional loving service to the Lord is not an activity of this material world ; it is part of the spiritual world, where eternity, bliss and knowledge predominate. The best way to begin devotional loving service is to try to offer everything you do, or some portion of everything you do, to Krishna. Any activities which are not favourable to the transcendental favour of the Lord Shri Krishna can't be accepted as devotional service. It is a natural instinct for every soul and can be cultivated by associating with those who are already fixed in devotional loving service.

- According to Shri Prahlada Maharaja, there are nine distinct processes of performing devotional loving service as Bhagavat-Cultute :

(1) Sravanam ----Hearing the holy name and glories of Krishna

(2) Kirtanam---- Chanting Krishna's name and glories.

(3) Smaranam---- Reminiscing the Lord's glories and pastimes.

(4) Archanam ----- Worshipping the Deity of Krishna.

(5) Vandanam ---Offering prayers to Krishna.

(6) Padasevanam -----Worshipping the lotus feet of Lord Krishna.

(7) Dasyam---- Offering physical service to Krishna.

(8) Sakhyam---- Becoming friendship with the Lord and

(9) Atma Nivedanam -----Surrendering everything to Lord Krishna.

Further characteristics of devotional loving service are described by Rupa Goswami with evidence from different scriptures as Bhagavat-Culture. He states that there are six characteristics of pure devotional loving service, which are as follows :

(1) Pure devotional loving service brings immediate relief from all kinds of material distress.

(2) Pure devotional loving service is the beginning all auspiciousness.

(3) Pure devotional loving service automatically puts one in transcendental pleasure.

(4) Pure devotional loving service is rarely achieved.

(5) Those in pure devotional loving service deride even the conception of liberation .

(6) Pure devotional loving service is the only means to attract Lord Krishna.

Lord Krishna is all-attractive, but pure devotional loving service attracts even Him. This means that pure devotional loving service is even transcendentally stronger than Krishna Himself, because it is Krishna's internal potency.

TILAKA

* Tilaka is a mark generally made on the forehead and nose. Tilaka is essential for devotees, both for purification and protection, which is associated with higher consciousness and spiritual awakening. It is believed that by wearing a tilaka, one can connect with the divine and gain access to higher levels of awareness. Another benefit of wearing a tilaka is that it is believed to offer protective from negative energy. Further-more, it is a beautiful decoration that declares to the world identity of the wearer as a Devotee of Lord Shri Krishna. When people see devotees wearing tilaka they are reminded of Lord Shri Krishna and are thus purified. Sadly, some devotees, fearing ridicule, feel shy about wearing Tilaka. But those who boldly wear it all times --- even in their place of work will soon find the ridicule replaced by with respect. For applying Tilaka, various kinds of earth are sanctioned by scripture. Most devotees use gopicandana – a yellow clay sold in Vrindavan and Navadwip. Tilaka is generally applied after bath.

Devotees Wearing Tilaka

A devotee should not wear dirty or unclear clothes. Used cloth that has been washed and dried again is considered clean. Cloth worn while sleeping, passing urine or stool, or having sex is unclean. Cloth that touches anything impure such as wine, meat, blood, a dead body or a woman in her menstrual period is also contaminated. Basically the men devotees wear Dhoti and Kurta and women devotees wear Gopi dresses, Sari. The other some practice of devotional loving service as Bhagat Culture are dancing before him, singing before him, communicating his thoughts to him, offering him his respects, standing up and showing respect to him and his devotees, visiting his temples, reciting prayers and hymns in his honour, singing kirtans and bhajans, worshipping him with incense and flowers, offering sacrifial food, accepting the remains of food offered to Lord Krishna (prasadam), attending ritual worship (Aarati puja), and so on. It is also helpful to live in the company of devotees who have the same attitude and devotion to the Lord or seek their friendship and association (satsang). Acquiring the knowledge of scriptures such as the Bhagavat-Gita and the Purans is also helpful. Chanting the Mahamantra of " Hare Krishna, Hare Krishna, Krishna Krishna , Hare Hare :   Hare Rama, Hare Rama, Rama Rama, Hare Hare" helps devotees to connect with the divine power which gives them the potential to focus on the positives rather than the unwanted or worrying thoughts. In the world of spirituality and meditation, chanting mantra holds a special place for its powerful impact on the mind, body, and soul. The life in Goloka Vrindavan (Heaven) is blissful. It is above every material pleasures that we have enjoyed here on this planet, it more than what Vaikunth (higher planet) or any other Dham (spiritual world) can offer. There is no envy or hatred amongst the souls, everyone is happy in their own association with the Lord and is happy in each and every aspect of it. There is no darkness , no night time in the Heaven, it is always illuminated by the different planets and most importantly, the presence of the Lord.

(2) Christian Devotional Service

What is a Devotional ?

A devotional typically refers to a booklet or publication that provides a specific reading for each day. They are used during daily prayer on meditation. The daily passage helps focus your thoughts and guides your prayers, helping you tune out other distractions so you can give God all of your attention. There are some devotional specific to certain holy times, such as advent or Lent. They get their name from how they are used : You show your devotion to God by reading the passage and praying on it every day. So the collection of readings is then known as a devotional.

Using a Devotional :

Christian use their devotionals as a way to grow closer to God and learn more about the Christian life. Devotional books are not meant to be read in one sitting : They are designed for you to read a bit every day and pray on the passages. By praying every day. Christians develop a stronger relationship with God. A good way to start incorporating devotional is to use them informally. Read a passage to yourself, then take a few minutes to reflect on it. Think about what the passage means and what God intended Then, think about how the section can be applied to your own life Consider what lessons you can take away and what changes you can make in your behaviour as a result of what you read. Devotions, the act of reading passages and praying, are a staple in most denominations. Yet, it can get pretty overwhelming when you read into that book store and see row after row of different devotionals. There are devotionals that also function as journals and devotionals written by famous people. There are also different devotionals for men and women. It is a good idea to start with a devotional specifically written for Christian teens. This way, you know the daily devotions will be geared toward the things you deal with every day. Then take soon time to skin through the pages to see which devotional is written in a way that speaks to you. Just because God is working one way in your friend or someone else at church, does not mean that God wants to work that way in you. You need to choose a devotional that is a good fit for you. Devotionals are not necessary to practice your faith, but many peoples, especially teenagers, find them useful. They can be great way to focus your attention and consider issues that you would not have thought of otherwise.

So may we all continue to do good and love and support our fellow-man in our hurting world. But as even the godless want to be good for man's sake, the devoted servant of God is personally directed to do good for Christ's sake. The true Christ-following disciplinship is based on devotional to Jesus Christ, not in good actions we do on His behalf. Humble Christian service flows like a spring out of a humble heart devoted to the source of that devotion, Jesus. There is no outside compulsion led by the Spirit of God. We are in a good place if we're spiritually led on inclined to areas of service that just feels right and fill our heart with true desire to humbly serve. Thus, devotional services are a great way to get closer to God.

Christians

Christians wear different types of clothing depending on the country or region where they live and the sect to which they belong. Christians dress in a range of states. The only dietry restricted by members of some Christian sects is the practiced of not eating meat or eating only fish on Fridays during Lent. Some Christians also symbolically fast. Otherwise, Christians eat whatever foods they enjoy and have access to.

Ten (10) ways to keep Christ in Christmas :

(1) Give God one very special gift just from you to him.
(2) Set aside a special to read the Christmas story.
(3) Set up a Nativity scene in home.
(4) Plan a project of good will this Christmas.
(5) Take a group Christmas caroling in a nursing home or a children's hospital.

(6) Give a surprise gift of service to devotions on Christmas Eve.
(7) Set aside a time of family devotions on Christmas Eve.
(8) Attend a Christmas church service together with family.
(9) Send Christmas cards that convey a spiritual message.
(10) Write a Christmas letter to a missionary.

According to the Bible , heaven is a place where God lives, angels serve him, and his people live with him forever. Revelation describes heaven as a place of unending joy and the presence of God, with no more death , pain, or separation. It is a place of love, peace, community and worship .

(3) ISLAMIC DEVOTIONAL LIFE

*   The nature of Muslim devotional life in Islam is rooted in its basic theological presuppositions. The three primary fundamentals of religion are belief in the unity of God, belief in prophets and belief in Day of Judgement. For Muslims there is one and only one true God, who is identical with the God of Abraham, Moses, etc. The necessity of obedience to God's will is thus the foundation for all devotion in Islam. Every human being should aspire to live as a servant ('a b d) of God. For this reason, the required ritual acts for worship are referred to collectively as 'i b a d a h , which can be translated as either "worship" or "service." According to the concept of n u b u w a h, God communicates thorough prophets (n a b i s) and messengers (r a s u l s). Thus, human agency is essential to the process of revelation. Devotional life in Islam rests simultaneously upon the worship of and obedience to God, and allegiance to and veneration of the Prophet Muhammad, who serves both as a teacher and exemplar.

*   Devotional actions of Islam serve to transform the worshipper, bringing him or her into greator conformity with the divine will. Devotional in Islam is not simply an end in itself ; it is also a means for facilitating proper ethical behaviour. One who lives his life in the constant remembrance of God will develop the virtue of i h s a n

(beneficence) and become a more perfect human being. Devotional actions within Islam are thus simultaneously evidence of obedience to God and mechanisms for the spiritual education of believers. The most obvious form of worship and devotion within Islam are those actions commonly referred to as "the Five Pillars of Islam." These are : the confession of faith (s h a h a d a h), ritual prayer (s a l a t, or n a m a z), the fast (s a w m) during the month of Ramadan, the haji, or pilgrimage to Mecca, and the paying of alms to the needy (z a k a t). These are the minimal required devotional practices of exoteric Islam. Collectively, they are referred to as 'i b a d a h because they indicate and affirm the worshipper's stars as a servant (' a b d) before God. Muslims believe that God looks at people's hearts, not just their physical deeds. For an action to be regarded as worship, it must be performed with the pure intention of pleasing God. Therefore, the concept of worship in Islam encourages people to connect with God in every action they take, strengthening their bond with their Creator. In doing so, a person gains a sense of true peace that comes with carrying out their purpose of life. Muslims must give 2•5% of their annual savings to help the poor, the needy and the oppressed. This act of devotion acknowledges that all wealth comes from God and purifies the soul from material greed. Indeed Islam enjoys Muslims to lead balanced live in this world while striving for success in the hereafter by living righteously. Therefore, the concept of devotional service in Islam encompasses not only the outward religious duties, but also the development of a strong moral character, good relations with people, and striving for just and harmonious societies. Thus, devotional service in Islam extends to all aspects of life, transforming mundane tasks into spiritual ones. Muslims balance their religious duties and everyday responsibilities, aware of their accountability to God in the hereafter. When people ful fill their true purpose of worshiping God, it enables them to attain a profound sense of peace that results from submitting to the Creator, the only worthy of worship.

Muslims Culture

There is no dress code prescribed for Muslims. This is simply due to the fact that there are more than one billion Muslims around the world living under different climate. Islam stresses the relationship between physical body and spirituality. Generally, Islam requires modesty both for men and women in dress, with arms and legs covered. Clothes should be loose and the curves of the body should not be discernible, especially in public. Muslim men are also required to be modest in their dress and covered their body, however covering hair is encouraged during formal prayers. The Holy Quran instructs women to wear an outer covering and to draw their head coverings over their bosoms.

Certain foods that have been deemed edible and lawful by Islamic dietary rules are known as halal food, which means permissible. Halal regulations, however, are not geographically nor temporally uniform. Muslims are urged to consume everything. Muslims are required by the Islamic Law to refrain from consuming a number of certain foods. According to others, doing so is the sake of one's health and hygiene as well as compliance with Allah's law. The following foods and beverages are categorically forbidden (haram) in the Quran :

(1) The meat of pigs (pork)
(2) Blood
(3) Alcoholic beverages etc.

For devout Muslims, this also applies to condiments or food-preparation liquids like soy sauce that may contain alcohol. Ramadan is the Islamic calendar's yearly month of fasting. Fasting during Ramadan means abstinence from all food or drink, including water and chewing gum, from dawn to sunset. Ramadan is regarded as a month of "great benefit" which can be interpreted to include prayer, food, companionship, and commerce. Every Muslim is obligated to pray five times a day called Salah --- Faith (dawn), Dhuhr (early afternoon), Asr (later afternoon), Mughrib (sunset) and Isha'a (night) , always facing towards the Kaaba, worship place of Mecca, Saudi Arabia . In Islam , Heaven is understood to be a place of everlasting life. "But those who have faith and work righteousness, they are companies of the garden. Therein shall they abide forever. "(2 : 82). For such the reward is forgiveness from their Lord, and Gardens with rivers flowing underneath that an eternal dwelling .

(4) DEVOTIONAL SERVICE OF BUDDHISM

As the devotional service for Buddhism world there are four steps we need to follow in order to achieve the goal of true happiness :

(1) We need to associate with good peoples who know the teachings of the Lord Buddha and who are trying to follow them.

(2) We need to listen carefully to those teachings.

(3) We need to reflect wisely on those teachings and apply them to our lives.

(4) And finally we need to put those teachings into practice and lead our life according to their instructions.

The Lord Buddha found the only way to achieve the Nirvana (enlightenment) and introduced it to the world as "The Noble Eight-fold Path." No one can achieve this noble goal without practicing this path. This opens the way to overcome sorrow and lamentation, disappearance of pain and grief, attainment of the higher knowledge and realisation of Nirvana. The core of Buddhism, i. e. the Noble Truth of the Path leading to the Cessation of Suffering is this : it is just this Noble Eight fold Path, namely : (1) right view, (2) right intention, (3) right speech, (4) right action, (5) right livelihood, (6) right effort, (7) right mindfulness, and (8) right concentration.

Devotional services, also as pujas or vandanas, are one of the ways that people express their faith in the enlightenment of the Lord Buddha. We do a devotional loving service before the sermon every Friday. A devotional loving service has several main parts : ---

(1) Placing things on the shrine.

(2) Going for refuge and taking the precepts.

(3) Reciting for refuge and taking the precepts.

(4) Reciting the qualities of the Triple Gem.

(5) Chanting a passage of scripture.

(6) A Short guided meditation.

One way we show our gratitude to our teacher the Lord Buddha is making offerings. Of course the Buddha is no longer alive and does not actually receive these gifts. By remembering his special qualities as we make the offerings we develop a stronger sense of who he is and what he has able to do. As our faith in the enlightenment of the Buddha grows, these actions become more meaningful. Traditional offerings, or puja items, include flowers, fragrance or incense, candles, water and sweet drinks. On special occasions people sometimes offer honey and different kinds of medicine. It is also common to offer food items in the morning when a meal is given to the monks. The special language we use in our devotional loving service is called Pali. It is the ancient language that the Lord Buddha's teachings are written in. In the time of the Buddha as well as today, people bow, as we do, to show our respect and humility. We bow to show respect to the Buddha and his monastic followers. One word we say throughout the service is "Sadhu !" It means "excellent." You will also hear "Namo Buddhaya," which means "Homage to the Buddha." As we place the puja items on the shrine, we recite the qualities of the Buddha. Through this recollection we make the offering more beneficial for ourselves :

(1) Worthy one (2) Supremely enlightened (3) Endowed with knowledge and virtue (4) Follower of the Noble Path (5) Knower of worlds (6) The peerless trainer of persons (7) Teacher of goods and humans (8) The Enlightened Teacher (9) The Blessed One.

At the end of a devotional loving service we ask the Lord Buddha to forgive us if we have done some wrong to Him. Although the Buddha is not physically present in front of us, we have the image of the Buddha to request and remind us of Him. The effect of paying respect to the name of the Buddha is not diminished in our minds whether the Buddha is present in front of us or not. Mere confidence in Him is what is necessary and sufficient for us to pay homage. When we pay homage to the Buddha we feel that we are in front of the living Buddha. This feeling arouses our deep devotion and dedication to Him. Therefore when we request the Buddha to pardon us for the faults we have committed unmindfully, we humble ourselves and determine not to commit them again. Admitting one's faults becomes a sincere and honest confession. Observation Day is determined by the lunar calendar, falling on the full-moon day, the new-moon day, and the two quarter-moon days of each lunar month. The full moon day is considered to be the most important of all of them. On the observance day the monks and nuns living in a community of four or more, gather to recite the rules of the monastic order. Buddhists generally go to the Temple to pass the day and night, often observing the three refuges and eight precepts. Many rituals and ceremonies in Buddhist communities around the world as well as the daily practice for individuals begin with recitation of the three refuge vows : --- 1. I take refuge in the Lord Buddha 2. I take refuge in the Dharma (doctrine or teaching) 3. I take refuge in the Sangha (the monastic order or community). The Eight Precepts : -- 1. Abstaining from killing 2. Abstaining from stealing 3. Abstaining from sexual activity 4. Abstaining from telling lies. 5. Abstaining from intoxicating drinks and drugs 6. Abstaining from eating after noon. 7. Abstaining from entertainment and beautifying the body. 8. Abstaining from using luxurious furniture. They spend their time reading Dhamma (religious and moral duties) books, listening to Dhamma sermons, meditating and discussing the Dhamma

Buddhist Monks

Primarily, the Buddhist diet is based on three dietary aspects - vegetarianism, alcohol restriction and fasting. In Buddhism, harming or killing animals is a great sin. So, they generally follow a lacto-vegetarianism diet. So, they can consume dairy products but not eggs, meat, fish, etc. This diet strictly prohibits intoxication from alcohol. Fasting is observed as a practice of self-control. They abstrain from food and drinks from noon until dawn of the following day. The most distinct mode of dress in the Buddhist world is the robes worn by monks and nuns. Not only does the robe physically mark the monk as distinct from the layperson, but it also serves as a physical reminder of the monk's ascetic lifestyle. Robes are most often saffron in colour, although the range of colours goes from yellow to red, depending on the monastery. On auspicious days throughout the Buddhist world, particularly full-moon days, pious laypeople will often wear special clothing, usually all white, to signify their purity and taking of the five ethical vows. A Buddhist monk believe their primary purpose is to practice and preserve Buddhist teaching while living an ascetic life. When committing to becoming a Buddhist monk, the individual agrees to lay aside worldly comforts to pursue enlightenment. This means forgoing incomes, salaried positions, and material comforts to exemplify the Buddhist way of life to their communities. Some commit their entire lives to being a monk. Others serve only a few months up to a few years. Historically, the first Buddhist monks were homeless --- before the days of monasteries. Their only possessions were their robes and begging bowls. Today, monks live in temple complexes funded by donation from the community. Giving alms to Buddhist monks is believed to foster a spiritual connection between monks and the lay Buddhist. The community believes they bear the responsibility to care for the physical needs of monks, and monks are expected to care for the spiritual needs of the community in return. Monks are a conduit through which a Buddhist can earn merit. A Buddhist layperson makes merit by giving gifts and financial support to monks. As they empty their cup of sustenance into the monk's bowl, they received spiritual blessing from the monk. This almsgiving furthers a Buddhist's journey toward

Nirvana, or true enlightenment. In the Buddhism , the arrival of kingdom of heaven aims to eliminate the sin of human beings while the departure for Nirvana aims to leave behind bitterness of the mundane world . Heaven is a realm of heavenly beings that is not an eternal place but heaven is a place , a happy destination , and the two higher levels of existence into which one might be reborn as a result of past skillful actions and accumulated merits by their good and enjoyed after death .

REFERENCES

1. Vedic Literature Texts
2. Christian Devotional : Related Websites
3. Muslims Devotional Practices : Related Websites
4. Worship and Devotional Life : Buddhist Culture websites.

(J) BHAKTI-YOGA AS A DISCIPLINE TO MAINTAIN PEACE AND HARMONY

Define Bhakti-Yoga

Bhakti means 'devotion' or 'devotional service' or "pure love" or "divine love." So Bhakti-Yoga means to practice connecting with God, and re-establising our relationship with Him, through acts of love and service, or devotional loving service. Bhakti is not what we do or have but what we are. And walking up to realise that --- is Bhakti-Yoga. A realisation that everything is the Supreme Consciousness, nothing else exists. Losing the sense of separateness from that allpervading Power, losing the identity that is defined by the world, and merging, diving into the vast, endless ocean of a throbbing, all-encompassing Infinite Love. Bhakti-Yoga is the lively feeling of oneness with that Spirit. Bhakti-Yoga, pure devotional loving service to Lord Shri Krishna, is the highest and most expedient means for attaining pure love for Krishna, which is the highest end of spiritual existence.

Philosophy and a brief introduction to Bhakti-Yoga

It is hard to define Bhakti ; one can feel it, realise it. With every breath, we sow the seeds of Bhakti. It is that love that sweeps us, soars us, and changes us forever, touching the deepest core of our existence. Bhakti is not about seeking that love but dropping the barriers we have built within, against it. It opens the door to eternity, within us. It is the love that shines in our eyes as the light of our soul. Bhakti wakes us to realise that everything is a reflection of the Divine.

History of Bhakti-Yoga

Bhakti as a form of union with the infinite must be as old as human civilisation. Formally it go recognized as a way of expressing love for the Infinite, or God, in Shvetashvatara Upanishad. Much later in Bhagavat-Gita, it was considered a "marga" or a path to realizing the

Ultimate Truth. It is elucidated further in Bhagavatam, as aphorisms made by Narada, in Narada Bhakti Sutra.

Flavours of Bhakti

The love towards God has various expressions or "bhave." They are :

(1) Shanta where the devotee does not express himself or herself too much, through singing or euphonic dancing but remains blissful and calm.

(2) Dasya Serving the Infinite as his most faithful servant, like Hanuman.

(3) Vatsalya Loving God like one's child, like Yashoda.

(4) Sakhya Loving the Infinite like a friend, Arjuna or Udhava are shining example.

(5) Madhurya or Kanta This is the highest form of Bhakti, where God is one's lover, spouse, beloved. One achieves complete oneness with the beloved. Radha displayed this love, as did Meera or the Gopies of Vrindavan.

Bhakti (Path of Devotion)

In Bhakti, one can experience total freedom from fear and worry. A devotee transcends worldly sorrows and pains. A pure devotee has no selfish desires, including the desire for liberation. Bhakti in one's heart is kindled by the grace of the Guru (spiritual master), by being in the company of other devotees and reading and listening to the stories of other "bhakta" or "devotee".

Bhagavat-Gita : Attaining Peace and Harmony with Devotion

Arjuna sought refuge in devotional loving service to Lord Shri Krishna, and that is the right path for peace and harmony. It's explained in Bhagavat-Gita that as sun is situated in one place but is illuminating the whole universe, similarly our little soul is illuminating the whole body by consciousness. We should try to make this consciousness a divine Consciousness. For that let us take small Spiritual steps which can help us maintain peace and harmony in minds and add a new meaning to our lives. Bhagavat-Gita is the essence of Vedic Knowledge. It is one of the most important Upanishads in Vedic literature. The speaker of Bhagavat-Gita is Lord Shri Krishna. The Lord establishes himself as the supreme personality of Godhead in Bhagavat-Gita. So we should take Bhagavat-Gita as it is directed by Lord himself. Bhagavat-Gita is the knowledge that the Lord Shri Krishna gave to his devotee Arjuna. Lord shared the divine knowledge with Arjuna because he was Shri Krishna's friend and a great devotee. So here it can be concluded that Bhagavat-Gita is best understood by a devotee of Lord. Without devotion (bhakti) it's difficult to understand the deep subject matter of Bhagavat-Gita. May be life poses hindrances to making advancement in this devotional path, but we should be tolerant and consistent to make our progress with determination. In today's world how can we be totally desire less ? But at least let's try to always remember in mind that everything belongs to the Lord and we should not claim false ownership over anything. Ultimately everybody strives for peace and harmony in his / her life. The real peace can be achieved with the grace of the Lord and Bhagavat-Gita, Lord himself is directing us not to be carried away by the incessant desires. Let's try to make Bhakti a part of our daily routine. Activity in the mode of pure goodness is called bhakti, or devotional loving service to the Supreme Person. Bhakti is both means and end. As the means, the practice of bhakti cleanses us of false ego and revives our pure consciousness that we are eternal servants of Krishna. As the end, bhakti is the eternal activity of the liberated souls who are absorbed in love of God and have no other desire than to serve Him.

According to the Srimad Bhagavad Gita , peace is a state of perfect tranquility and freedom from suffering . It is achieved through the practice of self - realization , which is the knowledge that the true self is not the body or mind , but the soul . The soul is eternal , unchanging , and blissful . When we realize the true nature of the self , we are liberated from the cycle of birth and death , and we experience peace . Thus it is about understanding how we can overcome difficulty , self - doubt , and ultimately live a life of truth and purpose . The power of God is with you at all times ; through the activities of mind , senses , breathing , and emotion ; and is constantly doing all the work using you as a mere instrument . " Even if one is impious and has committed abominable acts , if he worships Me with one - pointed devotion , such a person should be considered saintly because his determination is perfect . He quickly becomes virtuous again and attains everlasting peace in life . For this is my word of promise , that he who loves me shall not perish . " (Lord Sri Krishna) .

"When goodness grows weak , when evil increases , I advent Myself on earth in every age to deliver the holy , to destroy the sin of the sinner , to re-establish righteousness." (Lord Shri Krishna, B. G. 4 : 7 - 8).

REFERENCES

1. Vedic Literature Texts

(K) ISLAMISM AS A RELIGION OF LOVE AND PEACE

* Islam is "submission to God, accepting His authority as well as obeying His orders," "one's total submission to God and serving only Him," "embracing the messages of the Prophet Muhammad (peace be upon him) and abiding by them." In this sense, a Muslim is one who is under the peaceful and safe shade of Islam. God wants a Muslim to live in a safe and peaceful environment and to make efforts for the spread and continuity of peace. In order to be able portray a fair image of Islam, we have to consider its divinity inspired purposes, which yield, as a result, a just worldly order. By applying preventive measures to ensure security of wealth, life, mind, religion and reproduction, Islam aims to build a society in peace, serenity, friendship, collaboration, altruism, justice and virtue. According to the Quran, all Muslims are brothers and sisters to each other and if a disagreement appears among them they make peace and correct it (Quran, 49 : 10). Since God and the Messenger of God are merciful and compassionate to believers, those who take the divinely prescribed ethics and the prophetic character as their example should obviously treat one another with mercy and compassion. Therefore, those who have received the Prophet Muhammad's (peace be upon him) message can never be severe, arrogant, antagonistic or hostile. Characteristics like language, ancestry, race, wealth and poverty are not signs of superiority. In Islam, the individual is considered as a person that gain value within the society, as someone who is responsible to the community in a social context. According to Islam, the life of a human being is a trust from God, irrespective of his or her ancestry, colour or language, and hence should be protected meticulously. The main idea in Islam is to praise God the Almighty (Quran, 1 : 1 : 6 : 45), to show compassion to creation. Human-kind is the best of all creation (Quran, 17: 70) and is created of the best stature (Quran 95 : 4). So, every human deserves respect by nature ; approaching them with lenience, tolerance, and humility is certainly virtuous. Hence, staying away from hatred and having a tolerant attitude is essential for humanity. God the Almighty

asks from the Messenger of God (peace be upon him) in particular and from all Muslims in general to be forgiving (Quran, 42 : 37 ; 3 : 134). Thus, God loves good attitudes such as spending and serving for the sake of humankind at all times under all circumstances, forgiving people, and avoiding something wrong when we become angry. Even if one has the right to retaliate in response to an evil action, forgiveness is more appropriate for those who are more pious. The Quran enlightens all humanity on this issue : The recompense of an evil deed can only be an evil equal to it ; but whoever pardons and makes reconciliation, his reward is due from God. Surely, He does not love the wrongdoers.

*   In a place where trust does not exist, love, respect and solidarity are also absent. The lack of trust destroys family, as well as social, cultural and economic life. For this reason, the Prophet Muhammad (peace be upon him) states that trust worthiness and treachery cannot exist together and asserts, "One, who betrays, harms, or deceives a Muslim, is not of us." He describes the ideal Muslim as thus : "A Muslim is one from whose hand and tongue people are safe. A believer is one from whom people know that their wealth and lives are safe." In Islam, the right to life is an absolute value : He who kills a soul unless it be (in legal punishment) for murder or for causing disorder and corruption on the earth will be as if he had killed all humankind ; and he who saves a life will be as if he had saved the lives of all humankind (Quran 5 : 32). If we consider the troubles due to the extreme violence Muslims were exposed to both in the Medinan and Meccan periods, we can understand how meaningful was this message expressed by the Prophet. It does not include any desire for revenge against any person or any group ; instead, it only expresses an ardent desire for a violence-free world for all. The Prophet commanded us to maintain social solidarity and co-operation, to open our hearts to our fellows, and to help one another at all times. He said, "Do not cut relations between on each other ! Do not turn your backs on each other ! Do not grow hatred between each other ! O God's servants ! Become brothers and sisters !" The Arabic terms islah (reform) and sulh (peace) are from the same root. Islah means one's reach of peace and serenity while leaving conflicts and deviations ; in other words, it refers to leaving confusion by setting a dispute between two people or

two sides. Good deeds are actions that are beneficial for people and society, as well as actions that are taken to establish peace and serenity. This concept not only includes offering worship and spending in a good cause but also smiling, behaving warmly to others, establishing friendships, pleasing people by kind words, exchanging greetings, having warm conversation, and controlling bad feeling such as pride, arrogance, anger, envy, animosity, hypocrisy, rancour, and burning ambition. Thus, essentially, virtuous deeds are acts that purify humankind of aggression and bring them to peace. In the Qur'an, it is recommended to cease disagreements by peace and not to commerce further disputes, fights, confusion, and discord ; in addition, people are asked to take a balanced approach and seek justice. It is forbidden to spoil peace and tranquillity by corruption ; there are penalties for those who do. It is possible to apply the verse, Peace is better which was specifically revealed to eradicate disagreements between couples, to all kinds of human relations. Islam recommends a united and mutually helpful society, and this vision perspective, international law should take the establishment of peace as a foundation.

*   Peace is one of the major things in Islam and everything is done in the name of Allah (God) to reach peace. In Islam, praying and fasting for example is for inner peace. Everything is done for peace and as mentioned, It's one of Allah's (God's) names. Peace is the pinnacle of the Muslim paradise. God (Allah) is peace. The Messenger of Allah' Sallallahu Alaihi Wasallam ' said," You will not enter Paradise until you believe, and you will not believe until you love one another. Shall I inform you of something which, if you do, you will love one another ? give greetings (Peace) amongst yourselves. "If the enemy is inclined towards peace, make peace with them. And put your trust in Allah. Indeed, He 'alone' is the All-Hearing, All-Knowing. In heaven, Qur'an 56: 90 - 91 promises." And they are among the companions of the right hand, then they will be. greeted, 'Peace be to you, 'by the companions of the right hand." Heaven, a repository of human aspirations, is depicted by the Qur'an as suffused by peace. In 50 : 34, the Qur'an says that the virtuous admitted to paradise are greeted by the angels with the saying, " Enter in peace !' That is the day of eternity. "Therein they will hear no

abusive speech, nor any talk of sin, only the saying," Peace, Peace." (The Noble Qur'an 56 : 25 - 26). Allahumma Antas - Salam wa minkas - salam. Tabarakta ya Zal - jalali wali - ikram. O Allah, You are As - Salam (Peace), From You is all peace, blessed are You O Possessor of majesty and honour.

Qur'an 59 : 23 discloses that peace is one of the names of Allah Himself : "He is God other than whom there is no god, the King, the Holy, the Peace, the Defender, the Guardian, the Mighty, the Omnipotent the Supreme . "

REFERENCE

1. Islamic Concept of Peace Some related websites.

(L) PEACE WITH GOD AS CHRISTIANITY

* According to the Bible, the peace of God, "Which transcends all understanding." is the harmony and calmness of body, mind, and spirit trusting in the power and grace of God. The Bible uses "peace" in two ways. There is personal peace with God which comes when a person accepts Jesus Christ as Saviour. Then, there is the peace of God which is available on a daily basis as the believer participates in the Christian way of life according to the Plan of God. Peace with God is never available apart from Grace. The Cross of Christ is the focal point of Grace and is the source of Peace. Jesus Christ is our eternal Peace. Romans 5 : 1 "Therefore, being justified by faith, we have peace with God through our Lord Jesus Christ." Grace removed the Barrier and made peace between man and God. So, when the unbeliever responds to Grace by faith, the result is Peace. In the Christian Way of life, peace comes through fellowship with God and daily growth, advancement in spiritual things which brings stability, a relaxed mental attitude, orientation to the plan of God, occupation with Christ, and the ability to employ faith-rest principles in all areas of life. Philippians 4 : 6 : 9, Peace, or tranquillity, precedes the enjoyment of prosperity. It is part of the preparation for prosperity. One must have Peace to have the capacity for prosperity. God may hold prosperity back until there is the capacity to enjoy it. Jeremiah 29 : 1 7, Any loss of peace is followed by adjustment to the plan of God (confession and restoration to fellowship), faith-rest, and relaxed mental attitude, and Peace in the new situation. The man and woman who receive grace and peace from the Lord is in perfect position for spiritual production and reproduction. Jesus Christ's teachings and practices are very clear when we honestly read the four Gospel accounts. Christ's followers are to demonstrate love for others - and one major way we are to demonstrate love is through a life of peace and nonviolence. Jesus Christ wants His followers to put their trust in Him for protection and to be noted for their peace and love for others ! The kingdom of God, the focus of Jesus Christ's message, is all about how Jesus will bring peace to the world.

* Christian understanding of world peace must start with to teaching of Jesus of Nazareth himself. In his Sermon on the Mount, recorded in the Gospel of Matthew Chapter 5, he enunciated eleven categories of those blessed in God's sight - the 'Beatitudes.' They include "Blessed are those

hunger and thirst for righteousness, for they shall be satisfied" (verse 6) and "Blessed are the pure in heart, for they shall see God" (verse 8). Among those special categories of blessedness are peacemakers : "Blessed are the peace-makers, for they shall be called children of God" (verse 9). Jesus declared that those dedicated to overcoming conflicts and making peace between individuals, within and between families, in the wider society, and between the nations of humanity, are both blessed by God and especially close and dear to him, as children to a father. If we why this should be so, it is because the ' grand narrative ' of Christian theology tells of humanity dwelling in an ideal ' Garden of Eden ' in peace and harmony among one another, with Nature and with the Creator God. However one interprets the Genesis story for me it is symbolic for all time, rather than literally for a specific prehistory time - this is clear : The divine purpose for humanity is peace and harmony, but this is frustrated by human rebellion against God's purpose, in wars and conflicts. So Jesus said those who strive to achieve God's peaceful purposes for humanity are blessed, and God's children, acting in line with the divine will. Attaining great importance to peace as Christian Ethics : The New Testament in fact does not present a new code of ethical behaviour, but it emphasizes a new motive for it. A large part of Jesus's teachings was ethical. When an earnest young man asked him, "what should I do to inherit eternal life ?" Jesus answered in accordance with old law and said, Do not kill, do not commit adultery, do not steal, do not bear false witness and do not defraud. Honour your father and mother. Love your neighbour as yourself. Thus atonement in the Bible as Peace is a fruit of the spirit but the fruit of the spirit is love, joy, peace, patience, kindness, goodness, faithfulness etc.

* With living to the expectation of reaching paradise, all adherents are to live as peace-makers, worship their God by building and maintaining their relationships, treat others the way they want to be treated, and most importantly, contribute to world peace, which enhance the goal of achieving world peace as remembering some verses found in holy Bible scriptures. "Come to me, all you who are weary and burdened, and I will give you rest. "For God is not a God of disorder but of peace as in the congregations of the Lord's people." "They must turn from evil and do good ; they must seek peace and pursue it." "I have said these things to you, that in me you may have peace. "Do not be anxious about anything, but in every situation, by prayer and petition, with thanksgiving, present your requests to God. And the peace of God, which transcends all understanding, will guard

your hearts and your minds in Christ Jesus. Let the peace of Christ rule in your hearts, since as member of one body you were called to peace . And be thankful. Finally, brothers and sisters, whatever is true, whatever is noble, whatever is right, whatever is pure, whatever is lovely, whatever is admirable__if anything is excellent or praiseworthy_think about such things. Whatever you have learned or received or heard from me, or seen in me put it into practice. The Lord gives strength to his people, and the Lord blesses his people with peace. And the God of peace will be with you. Grace, mercy, and peace will be with us, from God the Father and from Jesus Christ the Father's Son, in truth and love.

Lord Jesus

"Lord Jesus Christ answered , 'I am the way, and the truth, and the life. No one comes to the Father God except through me " (Bible, John 14 : 6) .

REFERENCE

1. The concept of peace in Christianity Some related websites.

(M) CREATING PEACE IN BUDDHISM

* The Lord Buddha preached a doctrine which demands an in depth analysis of suffering and its causes as means of bringing about suffering's end and, therefore, of ushering in a new and lasting peace, tranquility and insightfulness. The most succinct formulation of the Buddha's doctrine was provided in the very first sermon that he delivered. That "First Serm on" set forth the Four Noble Truths of Buddhism, namely : (1) The Truth of suffering (2) The Truth of the cause of suffering (3) The Truth of the End of suffering and (4) The Truth of the path that Frees Us from suffering. The Buddha advises :

Don't accept something : -

(1) because you have heard it many times.
(2) because it has been believed tradior for generation.
(3) because it is believed by a large number of people.
(4) because it is in accordance with your scriptures.
(5) because it seems logical.
(6) because it is in line with your own beliefs.
(7) because it is proclaimed by your teacher, who has an attractive
personality and for whom you have great respect.

Accept it only after you have realized it yourself at the experiential level and have found it to be wholesome and beneficial to one and all. Then, not only accept it but also live up to it.

The Lord Buddha taught that peaceful minds lead to peaceful speech and peaceful actions. If the minds of living beings are at peace, the world will be at peace. Who has a mind at peace, you say? The overwhelming majority of us live in the midst of mental maelstroms that subside only for brief and treasured moments. Peace encompasses happiness and harming among living beings. In a wider understanding, peace is the nature and goal of every sentient being. Being peaceful is living in friendship with oneself and with every creature. Peace is indivisible but peril anywhere can be a threat to peace everywhere. Buddhism envisions peace as inner state of mental tranquillity which spreads outward. taining a state of inner peace by practice of meditation, which inspired him to work for world peace. In most of his teachings, Buddhist has phased that the practice of uproots mental defilements, which are, according to him, the causes of suffering and restlessness. Once a person overcomes suffering, he realizes inner peace. Inner peace projects itself outward, towards the family, friends and the larger society. This ensures peace and harmony in the outer world. Thus, world peace can be achieved through inner peace. Buddha became a source of inspiration to all humanity as he attained peace of mind. Buddhism has long been celebrated as a religion of peace and non-violence. To achieve peace within a person, the Buddhist approach is to observe and reflect upon the conditions in the external and mental operations, and then to decide on the most appropriate course of action as response to the outer and inner environments. With the most adequate response, we would not do harm to ourselves as well as not harbour negative feelings and thoughts owards other. Buddhism meditation is a call to divert one's attention away from the world of activity that typically consumes us and into the inner experience of thoughts, feelings and sensations. Meditation encompasses and focus which comprises the six forces : (1) hearing (2) pondering (3) mindfulness (4) awareness (5) effort and (6) intimacy.

Life centered on self naturally tends toward the selfish. Selfishness poisons us with desire and greed. When they are not fulfilled, we tend to become angry and hateful. These basic emotional conditions cover the luminous depths of our minds and cut us off from our own intuitive wisdom and compassion ; our thoughts and actions then emanate from deluded and superficial views. According to Buddhism, there are two kinds of peace, i. e., external and internal peace. The former implies the physical and verbal behaviours that are harmful and lead to killing, stealing, sexual misconduct and lying, collectively called the world's dilemmas which are opposite to peace. The external peace is the symptom of internal peace that means mental or spiritual peace, without which peace can, by no means, be achieved or generated. This is because Buddhism gives a significant emphasis on mind, as the leader or originator of actions and speeches, saying, "Mind precedes all things ; mind is their chief, mind is their maker. If one speaks or does a deep with a mind that is pure within, happiness then follows along like a never departing shadow." Buddhism has an intimate association with the concept of peace. In its long history we hardly find any evidence of violence, killings, religious hatred. Buddhism wields only one sword, the sword of wisdom and recognizes only one enemy i. e. ignorance. World peace, today, appears to be a myth, a mirage. However, it is equally true that despite diversity of race, religion, ideology and so forth, people all over the world are near unanimous in their basic wish for peace and happiness. Man hankers after peace because happiness is the ultimate goal of all living beings. and in the quest for happiness intelligent man finds that it is not available as long as one's mind is not at peace. As a social code, Buddhism leads us to peace, understanding and integration. Buddha tried to include in his followers the sense of service and understanding with love and compassion by separating man from passion to elevating humanistic tendency in man with the help of morality.

Buddhism is a gospel of peace and non-violence. Non-violence is a way of life devoid of all extremes of passion like anger, enmity, pleasure and pain. True peace emanates from non-violence which is a rational and mighty force. The practice of non-violence is life-affirming which contributes to human unity, progress and peace. Non-violence teaches one to live in harmony with others and with oneself. It requires adherence to high standards of truth and self-control. The principle of Non-violence projects an ideal of universal peace.

The Buddhism felt that it was imperative to cultivate right mindfulness for all aspects of life in order to see things as they really are, or in other words, to "stop and smell the roses." He encouraged keen attention and awareness of all things through the four foundations of mindfulness :

(1) Contemplation of the body
(2) Contemplation of feelings
(3) Contemplation of status of mind
(4) Contemplation of phenomena.

The Buddha's Teachings are so valuable. In the beginning as they point us in the right direction. In the middle as they make perfect sense, showing us what is right, what is wrong and we can verify the truth for ourselves. In the end as we truly wash away the impurities in our hearts and minds, and suffering disappears, step by step. Buddhism is an outstanding religious theological tradition a tradition of peace and harmony based on the philosophy of philanthropic humanism and universal fraternity which is a hallmark of Lord Buddha's teachings transcending all national racial social and cultural barriers. Buddhism believes in the potential divinity of the universal human soul. To Lord Buddha Dhamma is nothing but religious righteousness as the true guiding spirit of humanity. Thus Buddhism is the religion of peace as the enlightenment path finder and enkindled torch bearer for the universal mankind which is based on the noble spiritualistic mission "Live and Let Live, Help and Not Fight, Assimilation and Synthesis but Not Destruction, Peace Tranquillity Harmony and Happiness But Not Dissension." History has proved that whenever the universal, non-sectarian teaching of the Buddha has gone to any place or community, it has never clashed with the traditional culture. Instead, like sugar dissolving in milk, the teachings have been gently assimilation to sweeten and enhance society. We all know how much the sweetness of peace and Tranquillity is needed in the bitter world today. May the teaching of the Enlightenment One bring peace and happiness to more and more individuals, thus making more and more societies around the world peace and happy.

"Everything that has a beginning has an ending. Make your peace with that and all will be well. Whatever precious jewel there is there is in the heavenly worlds, there is nothing comparable to one who is Awakened. Be truthful; do not yield to anger. Give freely, even if you have but little. The gods will bless you. Satisfied life is better than successful life. Because our success is measured by others. But our satisfaction is measured by our own soul, mind and heart. There is no greater wealth in this world than Peace of Mind. Resolutely train yourself to attain Peace. If you truly loved yourself, you could never hurt another. Be where you are; otherwise you will miss your life. All that we are is the result of what we have thought. Three things cannot be long hidden; the sun, the moon, and the truth. Happiness will never come to those who fail to appreciate what they already have. Pain is inevitable. Suffering is optional. Purity or impurity depends on oneself, one can purify another. One moment can change a day ,one day can change a life, and one life can change the world." (Lord Buddha). Namo Amida Buddha. O Blessed One.

Shakyamuni Buddha, Precious treasury of compassion, Bestower of supreme inner peace, You, who love all beings without exception, Are the source of happiness and goodness ; And you guide us to the liberating path.

May all beings be happy
May all beings be peaceful
May all beings be liberated.

Lord Buddha

"The root of suffering is attachment." "Nothing is forever except change." "Do not look for a sanctuary in anyone except yourself." "If you find no one to support you on the spiritual path, walk alone." (Lord Buddha).

REFERENCE

1. The Philosophy of Buddhism Some Related Websites.

(N) LAWS OF NATURE : THE PERFECTION IN LIFE

* The first and most foundational law of the universe is the law of Divine Oneness, which highlights the interconnectedness of all things. It says that beyond our senses, every thought, action, and event is in some way connected to anything and everything else. The natural laws of the universe (cosmic law) as the law of cause and effect states that for every action, there is an equal and opposite reaction. Every cause has an effect and every effect has a cause. Be at cause for what you desire, and you will get the effect. All thoughts is creative, so be careful what you wish for - you will get it. The laws of Nature are very different from the laws of man. While the laws of man seek to order and control individual and social behaviour so as to make communal life less risky, the laws of Nature are deduced from long term observation of repeatable patterns and trends. While the laws of man may vary from culture to culture, based as they are on moral values that lack universal standards, the laws of Nature aim at universality, at uncovering behaviours that are true in the sense of being verifiable - across time and space. Habit is man's second nature, it is very difficult to break. Thus, the laws of nature are very subtle and are very diligently administered, although people do not know it. In the Manu-samhita (the Vedic law book for mankind) the concept of a life for a life is sanctioned, and it is actually observed throughout the world. Similarly, there are other laws which state that one cannot even kill an ant without being responsible. Since we cannot create, we have no right to kill any living entity, and therefore man-made laws that distinguish between killing a man and killing an animal are important. Although there are imperfections in man-made laws there cannot be defects in the laws of God. According to the laws of God, killing an animal is as punishable as killing a man. Those who draw distinctions between the two are concocting their own laws. In Bhagavad-gita God declares that all 84,00,000 species of living entities are His sons. "And I am their seed-giving father," the Lord says. Just as in ordinary material procreation the father gives the seed and the mother

develops the body by supplying the necessary blood to the embryo, similarly, the living entities, parts and parcels of the supreme father, are impregnated by the Lord in material nature. The dimension of the spirit soul is minute and is given in the scriptures as kesagra - one ten thousandth the portion of the tip of a hair. The dimension of the spiritual sparks is so minute that is invisible to mundane vision. All of this information is given in the scriptures, but because we do not have the proper vision, we cannot see. Although our material eyes cannot perceive the nonetheless within the body, and as soon as it departs, it takes another body according to this work. One should always consider that behind all these activities is superior superintendence. Now we have human bodies, but in the next life we may not have them ; we may have something else, better or lower. The type of body is decided by the living entity's superiors. Generally the living entity does not know the science of how the spirit soul transmigrates from one body to another. The spirit soul transmigrates even in the duration of one life as the body changes. When the body is first manifest in the womb of the mother, it is very small, just like a pea, and it gradually develops nine holes --- two eyes, two ears, two nostrils, one mouth, one genital, and one rectum. In this way the body develops, and as long as it needs to develop within the mother's womb, it remains there. When it is sufficiently developed to go outside, it comes out and grows. Growth entails changing of the body. This change cannot be understood because it is imperceivable to the living entity. In childhood we had small bodies which now no longer exist ; therefore it can be said that we have changed our bodies. Similarly, because of the nature of material things, we have to change this body when it ceases to work. Every material thing deteriorates, and like a broken machine or an old piece of cloth the body becomes useless after a certain length of time.

*   Although this process of growth is always taking place, the educational system in modern universities, through considered advanced, unfortunately does not deal with this. Actually there is no education without spiritual knowledge. One can learn to earn bread, eat, sleep and mate without a formal education. Animals are not educated they are not technicians, and they are also eating, sleeping, mating and defending. If

the educational system simply teaches these processes, it does not deserve the name of education. Real education enables us to understand what we are. As long as man does not develop his consciousness by understanding the truth of the self, all of his actions will be performed in the mode of ignorance. A human life is meant, for victory over the laws of material nature. Actually, we are all trying to attain that victory in order to counteract the onslaught of material nature. The ultimate victory is to conquer birth, death, disease and old age, but we have neglected system death with the proper utilisation of what God is supplying, it would improve. All the fruits and grains we eat are given by God, who supplies food to all living entities. One living entity is food for another. Animals without hands are food for animals with hands, such as ourselves. Animals with no legs are food for animals with four legs. Grass is a living entity, but it has no legs with which to move, and thus it is eaten by cows and other animals. Such non-moving entities are food for moving animals, and in this way the world is a constant struggle between exploiters and exploited. The weaker is exploited by the stronger ; this is a nature's law. We are integral with God, because we are part and parcel of God, our relationship with God is eternal. That relationship simply has to be revived, and that revived is this process of devotion. Human life is very precious in God's sacred creation. We should respect one another and should cultivate unity while allowing for diversity. We are all eternal spiritual beings and the ultimate good of human life is to achieve love of the Supreme God. At present we are under sway of different concepts. One person is thinking that he is Russian another is thinking that he is Japanese and someone else is thinking. "I am God's." When we think in this way, we are thinking in devotion. Only in this way can universal love among all living entities be established. God is related to everyone as eternal father, and consequently when we establish a God conscious relationship, we become related to everyone. When one marries he automatically establishes a relationship with the spouse's family. Similarly, if we re-establish our original relationship with God, we will establish our true relationship with everyone else. That is the ground for real universal love. Universal love is artificial and cannot endure unless we establish our relationship with the centre. Our relationship with God, however, it is eternal and not subject to time and circumstance. When we re-establish our relationship with God, the questions of universal brotherhood, justice, peace, and prosperity will be answered. There is no possibility of realising these higher ideals without God. If the central point is missing, how can there be brotherhood and peace?

* Some people even claim, "I am God," but they do not even know what is going on within their own bodies. The body is a bag of stool, urine, blood and bones. If one believe that intelligence comes out of stool, urine, blood and bones, he is a fool. Can we create intelligence by mixing stool, urine, bones and blood ? Nonetheless people still think, "I am this body." Therefore the scriptures say that whoever accepts this body as the self and children and family as his own, is illusioned. FALSE ego means accepting this body is oneself. When one understands that he is not this body and is spirit soul, he comes to his real ego. Even in the field of devotional loving service, there are many persons who cite many scriptural quotes in the parrot-like fashion, without proper understanding of the instructions, religious terminology, and injunctions of the pure devotees. They are simply hankering to receive respect from people for their show of "knowledge." But eventually their position becomes similar to that of this villager. If scriptural quotes and authoritative injunctions are not properly assimilated and digested, the righteous community never appreciates them. It is also not possible to be released from the clutches of maya, illusion, through such a parrot-like verbiage. Yet although love of God is being given freely and easily, people do not care for it. In every scripture and in every law book man is warned not to kill, yet no one is concerned with these laws. What is the remedy for this ? By practical experience and by hearing from authorities, everyone knows what sinful activity is, and no one can say, "I do not know what sin is." Every living entity is searching after peace. The conditioned souls within the clutches of illusory energy are all anxious to attain peace in the material world. Under the spell of illusion, living entities are trying to be lords of all they survey, but actually they are dominated by the material energy of God. The God is the master of material nature and the conditioned souls are under the stringent rules of that nature. Unless one understands these bare facts, it is not possible to achieve peace in the world either

individually or collectively. The struggle for existence concerns the competition or battle for resources needed to live. It can refer to human society, or to organisms in nature. Lord Chaitanya Mahaprabhu said that the only peaceful man is he who is in full devotional loving service to God, for he has no demands. He is a karmi, which means he does not suffer the reactions of his activities, that he has no desire, is self-sufficient and has nothing to ask. Such a person, fully situated in devotional loving service, is completely peaceful. This material world is a world of duality - at one moment we are subjected to the heat of the summer season and next moment the cold of winter. Or at one moment we are happy and next moment distressed. At one moment honoured, at the next dishonoured. In the material world of duality, it is impossible to understand one thing without understanding its opposite. It is not possible to understand what honour is unless I understand dishonour. Similarly, I cannot understand what misery is if I have never tested happiness. Nor can I understand what happiness is unless I have tested misery. One has to transcend such dualities, but as long as this body is here these dualities will be here also. Insofar as one strives to get out of bodily conceptions ----- one has to learn to tolerate such dualities. The human form of life is not meant for struggling hard to solve the material problems which even a hog, a stool-eater, can solve. The hog is considered to be the lowest among animals, yet he has eating facility, mating facility, sleeping facility, and facilities for defence. Even if we don't strive for these things, we will have them. Man is meant, rather, to find out the source from which all these things are coming.

* It is because we are in material bondage that we have so many demands. The masses of people simply want sense gratification, and those who are a little more advanced want mental satisfaction, and those who are even more refined strive to show some magical power in this world. All of these are in material bondage in different ways. Therefore a person who is in devotional loving service prays to the Lord : "My dear Lord, when shall I be fully absorbed in Your thoughts or Your service ? When shall I be simply conscious of you and free from all mutual demands ?" Being absorbed in the thought of God is not simply being absorbed in some abstract, concocted speculation. It is actual meditation

on the Supreme Person that is indicated. By such meditation, all mental concoction and desires are completely eradicated. A continual peace in the world is everyone's want, but no one knows how to attain it. The defect in the philosophy of the peace marchers was noted by the Archbishop of Canterbury when he said, "You want the Kingdom of God without God," If we at all want peace, we have to understand that peace means knowing God. We first must accept the fact that God is the proprietor of everything and that we are simply guests on this planet for a most one hundred years. We come and we go, and while we are here, we are absorbed in the thought that "This is my land. This is my family. This is my body. This is my property." We do not stop to consider that when there is an order from the Supreme, we will have to leave this home body, property, family, money, bank balance, land, etc. Our position has to be totally vacated. When material nature takes us in her grip at death and offers different kinds of bodies, she says, "Now my dear sir, you accept this body." In this way we are forced to accept an Indian body, Chinese body, American body, cat's body, dog's body, etc. We are not even the proprietors of these bodies, yet we are claiming to be these bodies. This is all due to ignorance. In such ignorance, where is the possibility of peace ? Peace can only be had when we understand that God is the proprietor of everything. Our friends, family and relatives are guests of time. When we accept this knowledge, we will have peace. It is the nature of man, or his dharma, to serve. Service is not only characteristic of man but of all other living entities as well. We often see animals serving their cubs, or ants serving their community, or bees serving their hives - that spirit of service is characteristic of all. We render service either out of a sense of love or a sense of superiority. No one can claim that he does not serve anyone. It is the prime duty of all living entities to understand that their position is to serve God. That is our real dharma, our real constitutional position. We are eternal servants of God and therefore we cannot possibly escape rendering service. If we are not serving God, we are rendering service to our personal selves, to our bodies, to our families, to our society, community, or nation. Just as liquidity is characteristic of water, or sweetness is characteristic of sugar, so service to God is the characteristic of the living entity. It is the basic ingredient and cannot be taken away. We have to understand that the dharma of service is intrinsic for the living entity. When the word dharma is translated into English, it is often described as a kind of faith, but in Sanskrit the word dharma does not mean that. Dharma refers to the inherent characteristic of the a particular thing, that which cannot be changed. A man's faith can be changed - today one can be a Christian and tomorrow a Muslim or Hindu. The essential characteristic of service, however, cannot be changed. This service is the perfect characteristic of the human being. It is transcendental, not material. Transcendental refers to that which is beyond this material conception, beyond the material energy. In order to attain the perfection in life as pure devotional loving service, we should worship God without purpose and without motive.

* One God, one God's law, nature's law, and we are all under that nature's law, under the control of the Supreme. So, if we think that we are free, we can do independently, that is our foolishness. We have to study first of all what is nature's law. We cannot surpass the nature's law. There is no religion throughout the whole world which is not connected with the word God. So religion means to understand God. But if we have no clear conception of God, then the religion is defective. Everything is in harmony. That is God's law. Everything is in Harmony, material or spiritual, everything is in harmony. Man-made law is imperfect but God's law cannot be imperfect. That is perfect. Therefore we do not take other's advice. That is imperfect. We take God's advice because that is perfect. Or God's representative's advice, that is perfect. Dharma means the laws given by God. Just like God has given this law. "We must die." This is applicable to everyone - Hindu, Muslim, Christian, man, animal, trees, birds, beasts, everyone. It cannot be disobeyed. That is law. That is God's law. We may be very much advanced in knowledge or so-called science, but because God says that in the material life we must die, we cannot avoid this law. That is called dharma ! Dharma means characteristic, that God has given this law that everyone should die, therefore all living beings' characteristic is that he must die. This is called religion. Similarly, God says that "You are My eternal servant. You must obey Me." That is religion. Human laws are imitation

of God's laws. We cannot directly accept the Supreme Being. We must accept the servant of Supreme Being, real devotees of the Lord, as our guide. Most people in this age are not very serious about spiritual advancement and cannot undertake rigorous, austere disciplines. Understanding how things exist as separate from God is of no value. The knowledge, wealth, fame, strength, beauty and renunciation of a man who is unaware of God are worthless. One must come to understand that all these things exist in the Supreme Lord and that they are His gratuitous opulences. By studying the opulences of God we can come to understand why He is worthly of our worship. We may adore the beauty, wealth, fame, knowledge, strength or renunciation of a person, but when we come to understand that these are only fragmental and that God is the source of all them, then we direct our adoration to God. Thus our thoughts should dwell in God. We can become completely satisfied only by thinking of Him, surrendering our lives to Him and speaking of nothing but Him. The wise are always so engaged because God is their all in all. Therefore the truly wise are the most opulent, for they belong to God and God belongs to them. God cannot be confined to the three (3) dimensions of height, breadth and depth, which are limiting this world ; but by His own inconceivable power He can come and sport with men as their equal and yet maintain His complete divinity. A person's mind is composed of two functions, technically termed sankalpa and vikalpa. Sankalpa means the mind's desire to join thoughts into concepts, theories and tableaus of theories. Vikalpa is the mind's function of rejecting thoughts, simplifying and limiting experiences which are gathered through the senses of sight, sound, smell, taste and touch. In this material world someone is enjoying and someone is not enjoying, but actually everyone is suffering, although some people think that they are enjoying, whereas others realize that they are suffering. Actually everyone is suffering. Who in this material world does not suffer disease ? Who does not suffer from old age ? Who does not die? No one wants to grow old or suffer from disease, but everyone must do so. Where then is the enjoyment ? This enjoyment is all nonsense because within this material world there is no enjoyment. It is simply our imagination. One should not think, "This is enjoyment, and this is suffering." Everything is suffering ! This cosmic manifestation is called nature, but there is another nature, which is superior. The cosmic manifestation is inferior nature, but beyond this nature, which is manifested and unmanifested, there is another nature, which is called sanatana, eternal. It is easy to understand that everything manifested here is temporary. Time is called kala - past, present and future. What is now present, tomorrow will be past, and what is now future, tomorrow will be present. But this past, present and future are the past, present and future of the body. We do not belong to the category of the past, present and future. We belong to the category of eternity. There is a spiritual sky, where there are innumerable spiritual planets and innumerable spiritual living entities, but those who are not fit to live in that spiritual world are sent to this material world. Therefore one should be concerned with how to attain or how to be elevated to the platform of eternity. The developed consciousness of the human being should be utilised not in the animal propensities of eating, sleeping, mating and defending but in searching out the valuable path which will help us get that life of eternity as Perfection in life.

* The soul is defined as a non-material, eternal spiritual entity present within any living being. The symptom of the presence of the soul within a body is consciousness. The soul continues to exists after the destruction of the body and it exist after the destruction of the body and it is existed prior to the creation of the body. The material body develops changes and produces by-products (offering) because of the presence of the soul within. The material body deteriorates in due cause of time and when it is no longer a suitable residence for the soul it is forced to leave the body. This is we call death. There exists, within this material universe, three types of energy : gross material, subtle material and spiritual. The gross material energy consists of earth, water, fire, and ether (defined as the space within the universe). The subtle material energy consists of mind, intelligence and false-ego (defined as the identification of the body as the self). The spiritual energy consists of the soul (the individual living entities) and supersoul (Supreme Lord who expands Himself). The presence of the soul in any living entities is indicated by consciousness. Although we cannot actually see the soul, we can see its symptoms. We cannot see

electricity but when we see an illuminated light-globe we can see the symptom of the presence of electricity. Similarly when we see consciousness we see the symptom of the soul. Any material body inhabited by a soul will undergo changes. It will be created, it will grow, it will produce by-products (offspring), it will dwindled and ultimately it will die. Karma means literally actions. It is described by the physical law that each action has an equal and opposite reaction. This universal law is not limited to physical actions, it works for any action. If we commit violence against another the reactions generated and we must experience violence upon ourselves in the future. This Karma or the reactions to our actions is not immediate. The karma is stored in our hearts and it will mature and fructify in due course. The ego is the identify of the soul. In reality the soul is a spiritual person possessing an eternal spiritual body full of knowledge and even increasing bliss. However, because of misusing their independence the souls in the material world misidentify with the material body. They think, "I am a Korean man, or I am an American woman." But such identification is false. We are only temporarily in a particular body. The living entity's fear of death is due to his false ego of identifying with the body. Everyone is afraid of death. Actually there is no death for the spirit soul, but due to our absorption in the identification of body as self, the fear of death develops. Matter is the secondary manifestation of spirit, for matter is produced from spirit. Just as the material elements described are caused by the Supreme Lord, or the Supreme Spirit, the body is also a product of the spirit soul. Therefore, the material body is called dvitiya means the second. One who is absorbed in this second element or second exhibition of the spirit is afraid of death. When one is fully convinced that he is not his body, there is no question fearing death, since the spirit soul does not die. If spirit soul engages in the spiritual activities of devotional loving service, he is completely freed from the platform of birth and death. His next position is complete spiritual freedom from a material body. The fear of death is the action of time factor, which represents the influence of the Supreme Personality of Godhead. In other words, time is destructive. Whatever is created is subject to destruction and dissolution, which is the action of time. Time is a representative of

114

the Lord, and it reminds us also we must surrender unto the Lord. The Lord speaks to every conditioned soul as time. He says if someone surrenders unto Him, then there is no longer any problem of birth and death. We should therefore accept the time factor as the Supreme Personality of Godhead standing before us. The Supreme Personality of Godhead is the cause of creation. As a woman cannot produce children unless impregnated by a man, material nature cannot produce or manifest anything unless it is impregnated by the Supreme Personality of God head in the form of the time factor. Since the living entity is constitutionally part and parcel of the Supreme Personality of Godhead, the Lord is very affectionate to the living entities. Unfortunately, when the living entity is bewildered or illusioned by the external energy, he become forgetful of his eternal relationship with the Lord, but as soon as he becomes aware of his constitutional position, he is liberated. The minute independence of the conditioned soul is exhibited by his marginal position. If he likes, he can forget the Supreme Personality of Godhead and come into the material existence with a false ego to Lord it over material nature, but if he likes he can turn his face to the service of the Lord. The individual living entity is given that independence. His conditioned life is ended and his life becomes successful as he turns his face to the Lord, but by misusing his independence he enters into material existence.

* The symptoms of the mind are determination and rejection, which are due to different kinds of desires. We desire that which is favourable to our sense gratification, and we reject that which is not favourable to sense gratification. The material mind is not fixed, but the very same mind can be fixed when engaged in the activities of devotional loving service. Otherwise, as long as the mind is on the material platform, it is hovering, and all this rejecting and acceptance is temporary. It is stated that he whose mind is not fixed in devotional loving service must hover between acceptance and rejection. However, advanced a man is in academic qualifications, as long as he is not fixed in devotional loving service he will simply accept and reject and will never be able to fix his mind on a particular subject

matter. Intelligence is the discriminating power to understand an object, and it helps the senses make choices. Therefore intelligence is supposed to be the master of the senses. The perfection of intelligence is attained when one becomes fixed in the activities of devotional loving service. By the proper use of intelligence one's consciousness is expanded, and the ultimate expansion of consciousness is devotional loving service. There is full co-operation between man and God and man and nature, and this conscious co-operation between man and God and man and nature can bring about happiness, peace, and prosperity in the world. The attitude of exploiting one another, the custom of the day, will only bring misery. Sometimes river flows very strong, sometimes it flows very small, but it makes no difference to the ocean because it is satisfied in itself with its own quantity of the water. Similarly, when our heart is cleansed with spirituality, we find pleasure and ecstasy with our own selves that is so sweet, so wonderful and so satisfying, that the so-called pleasures of this material world no longer have any values, no appeal at all. The human life is meant for attaining eternal and unlimited happiness by spiritual realisation. Human life is meant for reviving one's eternal relation with the Lord and all religious injunctions are meant for awakening this dormant instinct of the living entity. The human form of life is rare and valuable. We should know in perfect consciousness that human life is bestowed upon the conditioned soul to achieve spiritual success and the easiest possible procedure to attain this end is to chant or sing the holy name of the Lord Every moment is an opportunity to practically express our gratitude, and that is how we make spiritual progress. In this material world, to render service to the Lord, the cause of all causes and to see him everywhere is the only goal of life. This much alone is the ultimate goal of human life, as explained by all the revealed scriptures. The ultimate goal of life is to reach God. There are three kinds of illness : physical, mental, and spiritual. Physical sickness is due to different forms of toxic conditions, infectious disease, and accidents. Mental sickness is caused by fear, worrying , anger , and other emotional in harmonies . Soul sickness is due to man's ignorance of his / her true relationship with God. Ignorance is the supreme disease . When one banishes ignorance he or she also banishes the causes of all physical, mental and spiritual disease. When we understand our relationship with God then we all will be happy. It is an essential factor for establishing peace in the world. The beautiful material world is nothing but a shadowy of the reality, the kingdom of God. There are so many dangers in life because the material world is a place of danger. The spiritual master's order should be taken as the prime duty of life. If one gets a bona fide spiritual master and acts according to his direction, then his perfection of life God Consciousness is guaranteed. The perfection of human existence is to die to live. Everything is within the limits of time, but time moves under the direction of the Lord, who is therefore not within time's limit. Thus, true peace cannot be kept by force ; it can only be achieved by understanding God is the real purpose of life as the Perfection in Life.

REFERENCE

1. Back to Godhead (Journal).

(O) MIRACULOUS LIFE

* To make life meaningful and fruitful, we must understand that every seed that we sow today will give us a yield tomorrow. It is always important to use time wisely and carefully. Everything you and every decision you take today (now) will determine how your future will look like. If we want to live well, both externally and internally, how well we manage our surroundings and how well we manage ourselves. Fundamentally, life is management. The quality of your life depends on how well you manage your body, your mind, your emotion, your situations your home, your communities, nations, your life in general and world. Positive thought is an emotional and mental attitude that focuses on the good and expects results that will benefit your miracle. It's about anticipating happiness, health and success - essentially, training yourself to adopt an abundance mind set and cultivate gratitude for your own success and those of others. In the life a person, two forces of knowledge are operative from birth :

(1) the power of human reason, along with its satellites of sensation, perception, conception, and so forth

(2) the powers of intuition. The mind, body, and soul conception is a way of understanding ourselves as "whole people." A Whole Person has personal and professional lives that interconnect mental, physical, and spiritual components not only by influence both spheres but also interact with each other. In order to maintain miraculous benefits of our life as physical, mental and spiritual may analysis in different points of view as (1) Balanced Diet (2) Choice of Colours (3) Sleeping (4) Self- Talking (5) Why there is so much suffering in this material world ? (6) Never Stop Learning (7) No Suicide (8) Can Chanting the Name of God Remove Suffering or Past Karma ? (9) How to Utilize the Power of Prayer ? (10) Gayatri Mantra, etc.

(1) Balanced Diet

* A well-balanced diet provides important vitamins, minerals, and nutrients to keep the body and mind strong and healthy. Eating well can also help ward off numerous diseases and health complications, as well as help maintain a healthy body weight, provide energy that strengthen immune system, allow better sleeping and improve brain function. Opting for a balanced, adequate and varied diet is an important step towards a happy and healthy lifestyle. A balanced diet includes some specific healthy food groups under it :

(a) Vegetables such as leafy greens, starchy vegetables, legumes like beans and peas, red and orange vegetables and others like eggplant.

(b) Fruits that include whole fruits, fresh or frozen fruits but not canned ones dipped in syrup.

(c) Grains such as whole grains and refired grains. For example, quinoa, oats, brown rice, barley, and buckwheat.

(d) Dairy products such as low-fat milk yogurt, cottage cheese and soy-milk.

(e) The other aspect concerning the effects of healthy food corresponds to the natural environment we inhabit.

The importance of a healthy lifestyle : -

It is not balanced diet that's enough but also healthy practices of eating. Some of them are : -

(a) Eat-in smaller portions - You can do this by eating in small bowls to trick your brain into thinking it to be larger portions.

(b) Take time to eat - Not rushing your meals in between other work but taking the time to nourish your meals can send signals to your brain that you have had enough food necessary for functioning.

(c) Cut down on snacks - Unhealthy snacks are a strict no as they hamper your hunger. Switching to healthy bite - sized food can help.

(d) Curb emotional eating - Binge eating can be extremely harmful. Using it to relieve yourself from stress, sadness, or anxiety may affect your health. Instead, you can use healthier alternatives to best negative emotions.

(e) "Let food be your medicine and medicine be your food." Hippocrates, father of medicine. Using food as medicine means being responsible. Finding out what and why and how much to eat.

(2) Choice of Colours

How Do We See Color ?

There are two main sources of light that create the colors we see the sun and light bulbs. As you know, the light from the sun allows us to see things during the day as well as during the night when the sun's light reflects off the moon. There is a visible spectrum of colors that we can see in addition to the combination of all colors (white) and the absence of colors (black). Surfaces reflect and absorb light differently, which results in the colors we see through our eyes. The colored light enters the eye through the pupil, goes through the lens, then reaches the back of the eye called the retina. On the retina there are a bunch of light sensors called rods and cones. These rods and cones send a signal to the brain about what the eye is seeing. The cones are capable of seeing three colors : red, green, and blue. These are known as primary colors. These three hues cannot be mixed or formed by any combination of other colors. Additionally, all other colors we created by mixing these three colors. Secondary colors consist of green, orange and purple (violet). Secondary colors are formed by mixing two primary colors. Tertiary colors consist of red-orange, yellow-orange, yellow green, blue-violet, and red-violet. Tertiary colors are formed by mixing primary and secondary colors, resulting in the two-word names.

What is Colour Symbolism ?

Color symbolism is the use of color as a representation or meaning of something that is usually specific to a particular culture or society. Context, culture and time are certainly important factors to consider when thinking about color symbolism. Depending on the culture or society, colors may symbolise different things for different people.

Understanding the Meaning of Colours

If you understand the meaning of colors you can match your clothes to your intentions for the day or you can decorate your home in the colors that reflects your true self and what is most important to you. Colors and color meaning have been powerful symbols to mankind since the dawn of time.

(a) The Meaning of the Colour Red

Red is the most vibrant of all the colors. All other colors may be pretty and nice but red is vibrant. Many things which are significant to you are red. In human consciousness, colors have a big impact upon how you feel, and red creates maximum vibrance. Anything exuberant means red. Red is considered to be a color of intense emotions, ranging from anger, sacrifice, danger, and heat, through to passion, and sexuality. It's also associated with love and warfare.

(b) The Meaning of the Colour Blue

Blue is the color of all-inclusiveness. You will see in the existence, anything that is vast and beyond your perception generally tends to be blue, whether it is the ocean or sky. Blue is a serene and calming color that represents intelligence and responsibility. Blue is cool and relaxing. Light baby blue is peaceful while dark blue can signify depth and power. The color of trust.

(c) Meaning of the Colour Black

Black is the color of authority and power, stability, and strength. It is also the color associated with intelligence.

(d) Meaning of the Colour White

For most of the world this the color associated with purity, cleanliness and safety of bright light. It is also used to protect the absence of color, or neutrality.

(e) The Meaning of the Colour Gray

Gray is most associated with the practical, timeless, middle-of-the-road, solid things in Life.

(f) Meaning of the Colour Green

The color of growth, nature and money. A calming color also that's very pleasing to the senses.

(g) Meaning of the Colour Yellow

Cheerful yellow is the color of the sun, associated with laughter, happiness and good times.

(h) Brown Color Meaning

This color is most associated with reliability, stability and friendship.

(i) Purple Colour Meaning

This color is associated with wealth, prosperity, rich sophistication. This color stimulates the brain activity used in problem solving.

(j) Orange colour Meaning

The most Flamboyant color on the planet ! It's the color tied most this fun times, happy and energetic days, warmth and organic products. It is also associated with ambition.

(3) To Sleep Well

* Sleep is a part of your health and well-being no matter how young or old we are. Getting a night of good quality sleep has many benefits, which include protecting your physical and mental health, quality of life, and personal safety. The brain needs a good night's sleep for better functioning, emotional wellbeing, physical health, daytime performance, and personal safety. Researchers have suggested that adults need at least 7 to 8 hours of sleep every night to be well rested and be fresh and active the next day. Here is what a Good Sleep can do to Our Body : -

(a) Controls body temperature and metabolism.

(b) Keeping our immune system strong.

(c) Controls the brain function as well as help in restoring the memory.

(d) Keeping your heart and blood vessels healthy.

(e) Repairs tissue and stimulates the growth in children.

(f) Helps in regulating appetite, weight, and controlling your blood glucose levels.

(g) The adrenal glands also rest and recharge between 11 p.m. and 1 a.m. .

Here are the some miracles yet simple tips that can help we sleep well as wake up well :

(a) **Shower :** - The first and most important point is having a shower before going to bed. The human body is made of mostly water, therefore taking a shower helps to balance the body as well as calm down the nerves making you feel positive and fresh before going to bed and also help we sleep better throughout the night.

(b) **Meals :** - It's better to have meals three to four hours before bedtime, especially for those who have non-veg meals, this time gap is mandatory in order for proper digestion to take place. Also before going to bed and as soon as you wake up it's good to drink a glass of water.

(c) Keeping a Lamp : - Using an organic lamp with a cotton wick any oil in your bedroom is great. Keeping this lamps somewhere in the room while you sleep can create positive energy in the space where you sleep. You can also do a chant on prayer.

(d) Humans are Mortal : - It's important to keep in your mind that you are truly a mortal, believe that you could fall dead right now. It doesn't matter if you are young or old, you can fall dead right now. So, some sages asked everyone to go to bed thinking this is your death bed and you have just one more minute to live.

(e) Keeping things a side : - Last three minutes before going to bed keep aside everything that you have gathered in your life on earth - the body, the mind, things such as your phone, laptop, etc. It's better to keep aside anything that you have a personal relationship with. "Just sleep as life - not a man, not a woman." Once a person is successful in managing the art of sleeping like that, he will wake-up as a different person - more energetic, more productive, and more loving towards life.

(f) Placing the Head in the Right Direction While Sleeping : - East and South directions are the most ideal directions for sleeping. Sleeping with your head facing South reverses the negative effects of North direction and this protects you from several health problems. It keeps your blood pressure under check and also maintains a steady blood circulation.

(g) Try not to Wake up to an Alarm : - The kind of sound you wake up to can have an effect on your sleep cycle. Therefore coming awake to an alarm bell with a sudden start is not the best way to do your life. So what kind of sounds you come awake to will determine the context of the day. Once a person gets used to getting the right amount of sleep, you will be able to naturally go to sleep as well as wake up on time. So the best way to go about this is to go to bed early enough so that you come awake naturally.

(h) Our heart is the pumping station for your blood, our heart is what pumps life across the body - this process started from the life the left side of the body. Therefore, when you wake up it's best to roll to your right side and get up. Walking up on the left side is not healthy because when you are a certain state of relaxation when the body is in relaxation, the metabolic activity is low. When you get up, there is a certain surge of activity can be bad for the person mentally as well as physically.

(i) Wake Up With a Smile : Above all, it's important to wake up to a smile, which on the other side is only possible after getting proper sleep. Wake up with a smile because you are still alive, you are lucky to have a life. A Quarter million people die every day, and they too are normal people just like all of us - so being alive is really a great thing right ?

(4) How waking up at Brahma Muhurta help lead to Successful Life?

* Brahma-Muhurta is a Sanskrit word that translates to "time of Brahma," "sacred time," "time of divinity," or "the creator's time." It is the time period, perfect to perceive the ultimate knowledge. Brahma Muhurta begins 1 hour and 36 mins. before sunrise and ends 48 mins. before it. As we know that the time of sunrise differs with seasons and geographical location, Brahma Muhurta also varies accordingly. Brahma Muhurta is defined to be the best time to connect with the higher frequencies of the universe. The phenomenal change takes place during this time. This is the hour possibility which means that the seed of spirituality than has been sown inside you starts sprouting. After a good night's sleep, the mind is refreshed, calm and serene. There is the preponderance of sattva or purity in the mind at this time, as well as in the atmosphere.

Human life is a product of the several forces and phenomena that are happening around us in the universe. And thus human beings can function at their best only when he is aligned with the universal forces.

There are so many troubles faced by people these days despite they are all very intellectually and professionally acclaimed is only because they are constantly getting alienated from these universal forces. Getting detached from the higher frequencies gradually puts the human mind in a detrimental mode. The only antidote to this detrimental process is to wake up to the inner spiritual possibilities that lie latent within us. And that can only be possible if we try to be in sync with the higher frequencies of the universe. Thus, we can reach the zenith of our potential as a human being.

Waking up at Brahma Muhurta is best for health and longevity. The unpolluted oxygen you get at the Brahma Muhurta blend into the hemoglobin to produce oxyhemoglobin, that in turn enhances immunity and energy level, assists in maintaining the pH balance in the blood, and helps better absorption of vitamins and minerals. Invariably, having a healthy body ensures that you can bring out the best in everything you do throughout the day. That includes your work as well as your dealing with people around you.

There are a few things that people should minimize on avoid during brahma-muhurta to make the most of this spiritual time. Avoid eating or drinking, as it can disrupt the delicate balance of your life force energy. Avoid engaging in intensive physical activities, as it will disrupt the meditation state of mind you are seeking to cultivate. Do not use electronic devices, such as cell phones, computers, or televisions, since the light emitted from these devices can disturb your concentration and focus. Do not force yourself to stay awake if you feel tired or sleepy ; instead, take a quick nap. Additionally, it is also important to avoid loud noises and excessive talking as it can distract you from concentrating on your goals and intentions. Avoid activating on promoting negative thoughts or feelings, as this can interfere with your meditation and peace of mind. Try to maintain a quiet and peaceful atmosphere in order to get the most out of this auspicious time.

(5) Self-Talking

* One of the most powerful influences on your attitude and personality is what you say to yourself. It is not what happens to you, but how you respond internally to what happens to you, that determines your thoughts, feelings, and your actions. By controlling your inner dialogue, or your" self-talk, "you can begin to assert control over every part of your life. Your self-talk determines the majority of your life. The words that you use to describe what is happening to you, and how you feel about external events, will trigger the emotions of happiness or unhappiness that you experience. When you see things positively and you look for the good in every situation and in each person, you will become a very positive and optimistic person. Since the quality of life is determined by how you feel moment to moment, you should make it a habit to only think and talk about what you want and keep your mind off what you don't want. You are constantly faced with challenges, difficulties and problems every day of your life. They are unavoidable and one of the inevitable parts of being human. But as you draw upon your resources to respond effectively to each challenge, you grow and become a stronger person. When you look back over your life, you will see that you are the kind of person that you are because of all the difficulties and problems that you have had to overcome in your life. Without those setbacks, you could not have learned what you needed to develop the character and strength that you have at this point in your life. Much of your ability to succeed comes from the way you deal with life. Having a positive mental attitude is indispensable for success and happiness. It is the key to success in business, and it is vital to build strong relationship with other people. Everyone wants to be around a positive person with a cheerful attitude towards life. But no one wants to be around a negative person who is always pessimistic about everything. Your ability to develop and maintain a positive mental attitude, no matter what the situation may be, will play a critical role in any success you achieve. Here are some examples of your own affirmations :

(1) I deserve to feel good

(2) I am healthy and strong

(3) I have unique abilities and talents

(4) I take care of myself

(5) I feel safe and confident

(6) I deserve to enjoy time to myself

(7) I can make a difference

Some Important Positive Thinking as Miraculous Life-Style are following : -

(1) Except his own wife, he should treat all women outside, talking them as mother. Women should be addressed as mother. This is the etiquette.

(2) Other's property should be accepted as some pebbles on the street nobody cares for it. So nobody should touch other's property.

(3) Anger can be very powerful and can lead to being aggressive. Healthy people are not people without anger ; they are individuals who express anger usefully. We need to be able the handle our own anger so that there will be no outrage.

(4) What I feel, pains and pleasure, I must deal with others by the same sentiment. Therefore modern nationality means human being. The Conscious Mind defines all thoughts and actions within our awareness. The subconscious is part of our consciousness process that is not actively in focal awareness. The Unconscious Mind is a reservoir of feelings, thoughts, urges, and memories that are outside of our conscious awareness. The unconscious contains contents that are unacceptable or unpleasant, such as feelings of pain, anxiety, or conflict. The psychological technique known as Autosuggestion works by using self-induced affirmations that make it possible for individuals to steer their thoughts, feeling, or behaviour. They will subconsciously adopt a positive change and improve their quality of life. The power of Autosuggestion is enormous and it can be used in health, healing, prevention, relationships or career in a huge way.

(5) What is faith ? It is trust, assurance and confidence in God. Living faith is shown by service and obedience to God.

(6) Why there is so much suffering
in this material world ?

*   God is Omnipotent, Omniscient, and Omnipresent. Omnipotence means God is all-powerful. This means God has supreme power and has no limitations. Omniscience means God is all-knowing. This means God knows everything, including the past and future. Omnipresence means God is everywhere at all times. Thus God knows the suffering of everybody and can do anything or can remove the suffering from anybody, add to this God is loving to all. Why is there so much suffering in this material world ? If there is a God why can't He sees the pain and sufference mounting each day all over the world ? What is the purpose ? Questions like these tornment human minds all over the world. Science or philosophy or knowledge cannot answer this. The answer is given by the some ancient Sages and Seers of the world. "The purpose of providing experience and thus Liberation to the seer" (Patanjali). If you don't feel the deepest thirst, how would you know what is the joy of being in the light ? Experience the unwanted first, and then the unwanted will drop off like old leaves and the blossoms will come in spring of Life where the experiencer is the experience, where the marriage happens. The pain of separation and divorce is over !

People always want to avoid unhappiness, misery, poverty People always want to avoid unhappiness, misery, poverty, pain and enjoy uninterrupted happiness and pleasure.

But how can you perceive what is happiness unless you are ready to experience the opposite, that is pain and unhappiness ?

To be happy we need to lose happiness first. Then happiness has value. So don't avoid pain and sufferance, it is only on that black board you can write with the white the story of true joy in life. Life is a play of opposites. You can't getting one without the other.

If the Creator is perfect, and the Creation has done such a good job on us, why there is so much suffering in the world ? Why do we need to depend on somebody's compassion to exist here ?

It is such a perfect job, that it gives you the opportunity to be whichever way you wish to be. If creation has not given you the necessary opportunity to be what you wish to be then there would be no possibilities, is not it ? Then there would be no such thing as liberation. So, why create a bondage and then liberation ? Why could not we be liberated ? Then there would be no Creation ? Only because there is Creation, now the possibility of going beyond that ? Now in animal nature and in other forms of life that you see around you, every kind, there is not much possibility. The possibility is just to survive, procreate, carry on with life and die one day. Because there is not much possibility, there is not much misery either. You don't see other creature of the planet suffering like human beings. Their suffering is purely physical. If they are physically harmed, they are in pain. Even in pain, they do not know the kind of suffering that a human beings knows. Human being knows this suffering not because Creation gave this suffering to you Creation just gave you the freedom to make whatever you wish to out of yourself. You are making suffering out of yourself, or a large population of the world has decided to make suffering out of themselves ; that is their choice. Physical realities sometimes are comfortable ; sometimes are not comfortable. That is so. We have been given the necessary intelligence to create the necessary comfort for ourselves. That is not our issue really. If we have no problems with other, creating comfort for all the population in the world is not a problem. It is not at all a big problem really. Simply because we have inner problems simply because this freedom should have been a benediction, has been become a curse upon humanity. Right now, what human beings are suffering is not their bondage ; they are suffering their freedom. If you suffer your bondage, it is all right, but if you suffer your freedom, that is tragedy. Right now human beings are unfortunately suffering their freedom. This moment you can make anything out of yourself. You can make joy out of yourself, you can make suffering out of yourself. What to do ? if 50% of people or 90% of the people are choosing to make misering out of themselves. That is not Creation's fault. Just gave you the freedom so that you could go beyond. Once you have come as a human, you are not trapped anymore. Other creatures are trapped in their own instincts, beyond that they cannot think. You have instincts for survival, but still you have the possibility of going beyond these instincts. If you don't choose to go beyond, that means still enough suffering has not touched you, because it's unfortunate in the world that very few people transcend out of their intelligence. Most people have to be thrashed by life ; only then they will transcend. Only then they will think of going beyond, otherwise no. Because most people's intelligence is such, because they kept their brains in cold storage. They think they are going to use it in the future. So they can only seek anything beyond when something really goes wrong with their life. Till then, even if something really goes wrong, they will only pray for a better life next time. Now, you don't have to depend on anybody's compassion or understanding. The whole world can live under the umbrella of your compassion and your understanding. That the world lives under compassion and understanding, if you have any dignity, that's how you should live, isn't it ? Isn't it so ?

The gift of free will is beautiful and produces such wonderful pleasures, joys, and love, but with that comes the risks of pain and suffering. In addition, it comes with the risk that others also have this gift and may abuse it. These abuses of free will may very well affect a multitude of peoples, including the innocent and the righteous. In the end, it's simply a by-product of free will. In order to have the great joys and pleasures that come from the gift of choice, one must accept there will be troubles, pain and suffering ahead. But, it's those times of trouble that make love and joy all the more powerful.

When our plans fail, we just say "well, everything is in God's hands, we gave our best effort but God wasn't willing to do it perform" or "Man proposes, God disposes." This saying is a way of accepting the unpredictability of the world. We have a habit of attributing the unpredictable to God. "No problem what we hope , no problem how hard we try to execute that hope, the end result will not be in our hands." Nature is said to be the cause of all material activities and effects, whereas the living entity is the cause of the various sufferings and enjoyments in this material world (B.G. 13:21) .

All living entities within this material world has to face of threefold miseries : (a) adhi-daivika klesa (sufferings caused by the demi-gods, such as droughts, earthquakes and storms), (b) adhibhautika-klesa (sufferings caused by the other living entities like insects or enemies) and (c) adhyatmika-klesa (sufferings caused by one's own body and mind, such as mental and physical infirmities). The main problem confronting the conditional souls in the repetition of birth, old age, disease and death.

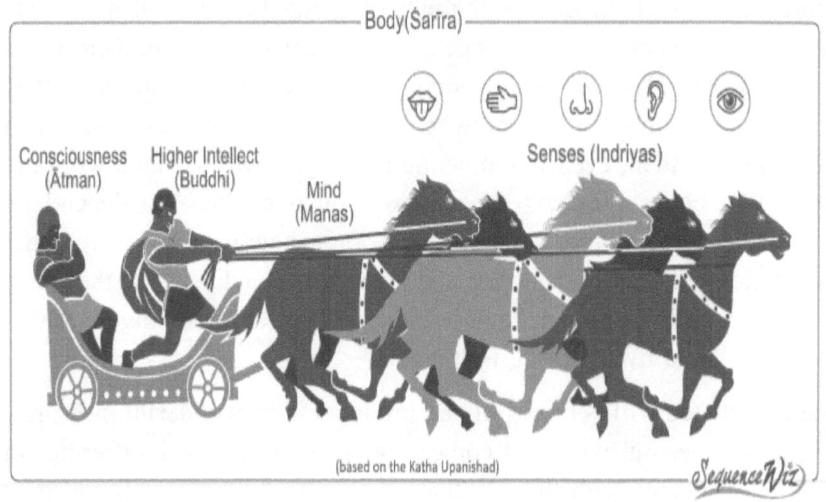

Five Horses riding as Mind, Body and Soul

The individual (soul) is the passenger in the chariot of the material body, and intelligence is the driver, Mind is the driving instrument, and the senses (tongue, nose, ear, eye, and skin are the five horses). The self is thus the enjoyer or sufferer in association of the mind and senses. The working senses are superior to matter ; mind is higher than the senses ; intelligence is still higher than the mind ; and the soul is even higher than the intelligence.

(7) Never Stop Learning

* It is rightly said never stop learning because life is the teacher which gives us the opportunity to learn new things each and every day. It motivates us to learn and defeat the challenges which we come across. The greatest teacher we could ever have is our life. Knowledge can come from anywhere and everywhere. All we need is to grab it and include that in our day-to-day lives. Many times, we may feel down but we need to

remember that it's not the end of the world. Sometimes, failures will force us to feel down, however we should never refuse to stand up, even if we will fall down repeatedly. We get to know a lot of things and these things become our memories, which are real lessons to the life. These memories could be good or bad, that doesn't mean bad memories are to neglected. Not at all. Each and every memory gives us a lesson to learn something new. Never think that we know so much, because that doesn't mean the end of our learning procedure. No one is perfect in knowledge. Each one of us learn step by step through life. Life will keep on teaching us every moment of the day, and we need to remain constantly open to change or take lessons from every situation that takes place in our life. There is no age or limit to which we can learn, whenever we want to know anything new, we just need to explore it. It only depends on us, on our real intentions, on our will to learn and discover something more, something new. Everything around us is lightning speed. This means that we also need to transform and adapt ourselves every single day. We should never stop our educational journey. Although we have done that, it's never too late to start learning again. Get excited about learning something new instead of getting panic and afraid. Get an overview of the things and there rules, regulations and system. Start the activity through the rule of "Just start." When once you started doing a little part, remove all procrastination, turn off social median and extra devices, follow the pomodoro techniques by setting timer. Take appropriate intervals to relax your mind. You should never stop learning as it enables you to :

(1) Improve your brain health learning is a brain exercise. You will avoid Alzheimer's disease by constantly using your brain and it will give you a long life.

(2) Banish boredom - learning keeps you busy and it helps you to spend time productively.

(3) Converse better - the more you learn, the more knowledge and ideas you can share with the people around you.

(4) Part of being successful is about asking questions and listening to the answers. Never stop yourselves from asking questions (Why, What,

and How), because curiosity is must in life to understand the world round us.

(8) No Suicide

* The body is given by material nature under the higher direction of the supreme Lord. Although we are proprietors of the body, still it remains the property of the Lord so it is not considered our property to destroy. Hindus believe that human life is very precious, which is attained after hundreds and thousands of births. It provides each human being with a unique opportunity to pursue liberation and escape from the cycle of births and deaths to attain immortality or make a quantum jump into higher planets of existence. Even gods and other celestial beings do not have such an opportunity to do so, unless they come down to the earth and the birth as human beings. It is therefore a serious mistake to waste such an opportunity by those who commit suicide to escape from their worldly duties and responsibilities or cause distress to others. It will not only hamper their spiritual progress but also delay their liberation for many lives upon earth. It also exposes them to greater suffering and possible downfall into the darkest hells. The immediate effect of suicide is that one is likely to be a ghost for some time. If you damage your body so badly that you die, you will have to do without a body for some time. Eventually one will take birth again and continue with previous karmas (deed and its consequences) plus whatever has accumulated during time spent as a ghost. The last resort of ghostly characters in human society is to the shelter of suicide, either material or spiritual.

(9) Can Chanting the name of God remove past karma or Suffering ?

* The Mantra (chanting) purifies the body. Man becomes pure by repeating the Mantra of God.... It is said, The human teacher utters the Mantra into the ear, but God breathes the spirit into the soul. May your body and mind become pure by repeating the name of God. The mind keeps well when engaged in work. And yet Japa, prayer also are

specially needed. You must at least sit down once in the morning and again in the evening. That acts as a rudder to a boat. One should observe regularity, however busy one may be with duties.......... Even in the minds of the most intense activity, one should at least remember God and salute Him. As wind removes the cloud, so the name of God destroys the cloud of worldliness. Do you know the significance of Japa and other spiritual practices ? By these, the power of the sense organs is subdued. Just see the power of habit. By the law of habit man attains realisation by continuous practice of Japa. One has to suffer the consequences of one's deeds. But by repeating the name of God, you can lesson its intensity. If you were destined to have a wound as wide as a ploughshare, you will get a pinprick at least. The effect of karma (past action) can be counteracted to a great extent by Japa and austerities. The conjunction of day and night is the most auspicious time for calling on God....... The mind remains pure at this time. What a lot of work I did when I was of your age ! And yet I could find time to repeat my Mantra a hundred thousand times every day! True it is that there is no hard and fast rule about the time of Japa, yet morning and evening are the favourable periods. Whatever the time be, you must do Japa every day. It is not good to forgo it any day. While performing Japa, take the Name of God with utmost love, sincerity, and self-surrender. When one sits down for Japa, God's name will continue rising up from the mind naturally and not with effort. The Kundalini (The Primal Energy Within Us) will be gradually awakened. You will realize everything by the repetition of God's Name. Even if the mind is not quiet, still you can sit and repeat the holy Name a million times. Before the awakening of the Kundalini, one hears the Anahata (sound within heart) ; but nothing can be achieved without the grace of the Divine Mother. One must cast aside indolence and meditation at the proper time. Prayer and meditation, or pilgrimage, all these should be done during the earlier part of one's life. Worship ends with absorption and meditation. Japa will eventually bring spiritual realisation. Pray to God with all you might. One has to work ; Can anything be achieved without work ? Even in the midst of household duties one must make time for prayer. Do not give up Japa even if the mind is unwilling and insteady. You must go on with the repetition. And you will find that the mind is getting gradually steadier - like a flame in a windless corner. Any movement in the air disturbs the steady burning of the flame ; even so the presence of any thought or desire makes the mind unsteady. The Mantra must be correctly repeated. An incorrect utterance delays progress. Spiritual practices are meant to keep the mind steady at the feet of God, to keep it immensed in His thought. Repeat His Name. One who makes a habit of prayer will easily overcome all difficulties and remain calm and unruffled in the midst of the trials of life.

(10) How to Utilize the Power of Prayer ?

*   In the past you may have been disappointed that your prayers were not answered. But do not lose faith......... God is not a mute or unfeeling Being. He is love itself. If you know how to meditate to make contact with Him, He will respond to your loving demands. To know exactly how and when to pray, according to the nature of our needs, is what brings the desired results. When the right method is applied, it sets in motion the proper laws of God ; the operation of these laws scientifically bears results. The first rule in prayer is to approach God only with legitimate desires. The second is to pray for their fulfilment, not as a beggar, but as a son : "I am Thy child. Thou art my Father. Thou and I are One." When you pray deeply and continuously you will feel a great joy willing up in your heart. Don't be satisfied until that joy manifests. For when you feel that all-satisfying joy in your heart, you will know that God has tuned in your prayer broadcast. Then pray to your Father : "Lord, this is my need. I am willing to work for it ; please guide me and help me to have the right thoughts and to do the right things to bring about success. I will use my reason, and work with determination, but guide Thou my reason, will, and activity to the right thing that I should do." You should pray to God intimately, as His child, which you are. God does not object when you pray from your ego, as a stranger and a beggar, but you will find that your efforts are limited by that your efforts are limited by that consciousness. God does not want you to give up your own will power which is your divine birth right as His Child. Prayer often implies the consciousness of beggary. We are children of God, not beggars, and are thus entitled to our divine inheritance. When we have

established a connection of love between our souls and God, we have a right to lovingly demand the fulfilment of our legitimate prayers. An unceasing demand for anything, mentally whispered with unflagging zeal and unflinching courage and faith, develops into a dynamic power that influences the entire behaviour of the conscious, subconscious, and superconscious powers of man that the desired object is gained.

Prayers for the Forgiveness of others : Forgive others and you shall be forgiven. Forgiveness can lead to (a) Healthier relationship (b) Improved mental health (c) Less anxiety, stress and hostility (d) Lower blood pressure (e) Fewer symptoms of depression (f) A stronger immune system (g) Improved heart health (h) Improved self- esteem etc.

(11) Power of Gayatri Mantra

* Gayatri Mantra addresses the supreme reality in the form of light. It does not talk of any one deity or god. Therefore Gayatri mantra is universal and highly scientific. It is common to all religions. It addresses the one single absolute energy or god whatever we may call the supreme principle that create, sustains and dissolves the universe.

Lyrics of Gayatri mantra in English :

Om bhur bhuvah svah

tat savittur varenyam

bhargo devasya dhimahi

dhiyo yo nah prachodayat

Translation of the Gayatri mantra

OM. Here's meditating upon the one who governs the universe, to illuminate our minds by eliminating ignorance. We meditate upon the Ishwar (God), one who sustains life. Enlighten us.

Benefits of chanting the Gayatri mantra

(a) Regular chanting of the Gayatri mantra shall help you focus.

(b) It helps in realising that there's a higher force working round the clock to help life sustain on the earth.

(c) It develops a sense of gratitude towards the universe that we all are a part of.

(d) By chanting the Gayatri mantra, one can rid his mind and body of toxins. Thus, the sacred Mantra helps a person in cleansing his mind and body.

(e) Chanting of the Mantra regulates the vital organs and helps in their better functioning. Nonetheless faith and perseverance matter a lot. Therefore, by chanting the Mantra with utmost devotion, one can reap benefits.

(f) Gayatri mantra removes all fears and diseases and enhances happiness, wealth and prosperity.

(g) Gayatri mantra contributes to one's spiritual maturity and helps the individual ascend in the ladder of spiritual progress through enlightenment.

All in all, it is important to understand that the Gayatri mantra is a true reflection of spirituality, and it is sure to help an individual in achieving everlasting peace and fulfilment. Nowadays, Digital Spirituality offers us a way to live on beyond our physical presence on earth, not just as a digital legacy, but in the forms of digital consciousness and digital soul.

When to Chant Gayatri Mantra

Gayatri mantra can be chanted at all times when you are working, travelling or resting. If you wish to chant its during specific times, the best times to chant Gayatri mantra are dawn, noon and dusk.

REFERENCES

1. Related Topics found in websites.

(P) INTERFAITH-DIALOGUE GLOBAL PERSPECTIVES

(1) Meaning of Interfaith-Dialogue

The term Interfaith-Dialogue refers to co-operative, constructive and positive interaction between people of different religious traditions and / or spiritual or humanistic beliefs, at both the individual and institutional levels. It is distinct from syncretism or alternative religion, in that dialogue often involves promoting understanding between different religions to increase acceptance of others, rather than to synthesize new beliefs. Throughout the world there are local, regional, national and international interfaith initiatives ; many are formally or informally linked and constitute larger networks or federations. The often quoted "There will be no peace among the nations without peace among the religions."

(2) The Role of Interfaith-Dialogue

The power of religion can be used as a major force of unification among divergent factions, and hence it can play a key role in the promotion of global peace and reconciliation, but bringing varying groups together in order to establish and maintain constructive channels of communication and sustainable collaboration. Interfaith-Dialogue therefore plays a vital role in the field of Cultural Diplomacy, as it can advance world peace by uniting faiths and by fasting reciprocal understanding, acceptance and tolerance amongst disparate religious communities. Interfaith-Dialogue can in this way break down walls of division and the barriers that stand at the center of numerous wars, with the objective of achieving peace.

(3) Need for Interfaith-Dialogue

It is the need of the hour that with thinking, feeling, willing, for the idea of World Peace through the Interfaith-Dialogue to be a good decisive mission so as to sustain spiritual life, love, respect, solidarity, and unity in the human society .

Dialogue between followers of different faith traditions has become an urgent necessity today. Undoubtedly, in today's world inter-community harmony is a major need, and the lack of it has emerged as a major challenge. Interfaith and inter-community harmony must be built on the foundations and concerns that different faith communities share in common. It must also seek to build bridges of understanding between these communities, and to eliminate misunderstandings that are a major source of inner conflict. It is also important to highlight the need for interfaith- Dialogue ; if they are to contribute to peace, religions should give some thoughts to how they handle manifestations of their own internal diversity, as part of a genuine culture of pluralism.

(4) Importance of Interfaith-Dialogue

Dialogue between followers of different faith traditions is very important to promote and propagate peace and corporation among different religions and cultures. Multi culture or the diversity in religions all over the world is an accepted fact which demands peace and tolerance. It demands mutual respect, mutual understanding and co-existence in religions and all the religions must come out of their choice. Almighty God has commanded not to use any kind of compulsion in the followers of one faith. It is not allowed to try to impose one's faith on others.

(5) Merits of Interfaith-Dialogue

(a) Interfaith-Dialogue demonstrates to the public how different faiths can live together in harmony without hurting of insulting each other's instincts. The attitude of dialogue should not be aggressive, it teaches the viewers and its followers that every religion and its followers must be given due respect.

(b) Interfaith-Dialogue can be helpful in removing the fear from the minds of the minorities who are oppressed and help them to cooperate with the majority community in the field of development and prosperity of the nation.

(c) Interfaith-Dialogue helps to explore and learn about each other and know more about the traditions of one's faith. Every person's inner soul is in search for a deep understanding of the truth that includes Almighty God, the Universe and the Life etc.

(d) Dialogue between followers of different faith traditions helps each religion to grow and develop mutually. Each religion through dialogue helps other religion for its enrichment. Interfaith-Dialogue provides space for the religion to contribute and complement each other. It helps society as a whole by producing better mutual understanding among the believers of different religions.

(e) Dialogue between followers of different faith traditions encourages in supporting of each other in times of difficulty. When natural or man-made calamities strike upon the society, dialogue helps in creating people and individuals who relief work irrespective of caste, creed, religion, language etc. They don't consider priorities in rendering their much needed services. They only see their services are rendered in its proper channel to each and every one affected by the calamities (the best example is during the pandemic Covid -19 in all parts of the world, people help each other irrespective of their religion).

(f) Dialogue between followers of different faith traditions is of great help to achieve common goals of the society and nation. It enhances the participation of every member of every religion in the development and prosperity of the nation. Dialogue help in making public opinion against the evils prevailing in the society and thus result in its eradication from the society. Dialogues minimize the gap between communities which in turn reinforces the national integration of a country. All human beings are entitled to participate in the activities that will shape the world in the third millennium. No nation should be left on the side-lines because of some philosophical, political or economic argument. It is not enough to tolerate world must be shaped by the massive co-operation of all human beings.

(g) All religions believe in selfless service to humanity. With the help of Interfaith-Dialogue, the services and aids can be extended to the people of other religions also.

(6) Disadvantages of Interfaith

Dialogue :

The disadvantages with interfaith-Dialogue is that conflicts that are lebeled religious are mostly based on social, political, linguistic, or cultural factors, and that the practitioners of different religions do not actually come into conflict at the grassroots level. In most current conflicts, fighting is basically not about civilization and religion, but about territories, raw-material, and trade and money. Hence, inter-religious dialogue does not focus on the core causes of conflicts and is restricted to exchanges limited amongst the elite. At a still deeper level, the sense of frustration, bewilderment or even anger which the presence of the convert presents can reach beyond the immediate context of interfaith-Dialogue to place a question mark against the religious identity of everybody in a multi faith situation. Religious practitioners have many identities apart from their religious identities which are not always based on "world religions." In an age when the religious are becoming increasingly disillusioned by organized religions and are looking toward nonconventional approaches to inner life such as the "spiritual but not religious." God , spirituality, religion and morality are all inter-related for peaceful compulsion.

Conflict arises when groups or sections of society try to redefine the dominant norms of society on the basis of which inequalities in privileges and power in society are perpetuated. As such, conflict may not be historical but a continuous process in social system . It may also be healthy for the social mobility and social regeneration in the system. Conflict may also create serious problems for the stability of the social institutions if it is not contained within the system through its reconciliation between the parties either mutually or by intervention of larger societal forces. Yet, there are conflicts in a social system that cannot be reconciled without completely altering norms or institutions of society. When such conflict emerges in a social system, we call it contradiction. Both conflicts and contradictions contribute to social change. Otherwise, the stability of the social systems would be in constant danger. It also happens occasionally that is why contradiction is a historical process .

(7) A Song for Inter-Religious Community Building in order to extend Love Peace and Harmony in this material World : -

1.

We are all spirit souls coming from Godhead
We are sons and daughters of the same Father God
We are one with God
All creatures visible and invisible
God made them all
Singing out all glories to Almighty God !

2.

Oh ! dear God, ocean of mercy
the source of energy in universe
We live to the heart of worship
We long to bring our lives many offerings
The path to peace is devotional performance
Singing out all glories to Almighty God !

3.

We are mortal human beings
in a transient world
Our faiths are the gifts from God
Forever we are determined to love God
And we surrender all to God
Then the God of peace will be with us
Singing out all glories to Almighty God !

4.

We are going back to Godhead
All our days with every breathing moment
We should remind birth, death, old age and disease
We should be kind to the nature
By the grace of God we will find inner peace
Singing out all glories to Almighty God !

In pursuance of Interfaith-Dialogue Aim is to systematically propagate spiritual knowledge to society at large and to enlighten all peoples in the approach of spiritual life in order to check the imbalance of values in life and to achieve real unity and peace in the world : -

(a) value charity, non-violence, spiritual education, moral thought and action, devotion, and service to God.

(b) value qualities such as humanity, tolerance, compassion, cleanliness, self-control, simplicity, steadiness, knowledge, honest, and personal integrity.

(c) value and respect the right of all other living beings, be they human, animal, bird, aquatic, or plant life. We value the environment and our natural resources as being God's property, which we have a responsibility to respect and protect.

(d) recognize the institution of the family to be an essential element in maintaining social stability and promoting spiritual values.

(e) our religious duties without to be disturbed the other communities is our real rights.

(f) internal peace and external peace are interrelated. Both are interdependent and help each other. Internal peace represents individual's peace while external peace represents peace in society.

(g) truth, goodness, and beauty are cosmic values that communicate divine meaning to the intellectual, moral and aesthetic capacities of human soul, which brings a balance in the soul, which, in turn, harmonizes the human person with divine meaning and purpose of the cosmos, which was considered the prerequisite to human flourishing.

(h) why are we called as human beings not as human doings ?

The Sanskrit word Dharma is sometimes translated as 'religion,' but Dharma means "essential characteristic." The Dharma of fire is heat and light, the Dharma of sugar is sweetness, the Dharma of soul is service to God. The essential part of the living being, that part which is his constant companion. That constant companion is his eternal quality, and that eternal quality is his eternal religion. A Hindu may change his faith to become a Muslim, or a Muslim may change his faith to become a Hindu, or a Christian may change his faith and so on. But in all circumstances the change of religious faith does not affect the eternal occupation of rendering service to others. The Hindu, Muslim or Christian in all circumstances is servant of someone. Thus, to profess a particular type of faith is not to profess one's eternal religion. The rendering of service is eternal religion. Factually we are related to the Supreme Lord in service. The Supreme Lord is the supreme enjoyer, and we living entities are His servitors. We are created for His enjoyment, and if we participated in that eternal enjoyment with the Supreme Personality of Godhead, we become happy. We cannot happy otherwise. It is not possible to be happy independently, just as no one part of the body can can be happy without co-operating with the stomach. It is not possible for the living entity to be happy without rendering transcendental loving service unto the Supreme Lord.

All truth is God's truth ,
All goodness is God's goodness ;
All beauty is God's beauty.

REFERENCES :

1. https : // en.m.wikipedia.org / wiki / Interfaith-dialogue

2. https : // www.researchgate.net /publication / Interfaith-dialogue - its - need - importance - and - merits - in -the - contemporary - world.

3. https : // readingreligion.org / the-problem - with- interreligious. Dialogue.

4. https : // vaniquotes.org / wiki / Dharma.